WOODWORK PROJECTS

Pine Furniture Making

WOODWORK PROJECTS

Pine Furniture Making

Anthony Hontoir

The Crowood Press

First published in 1993 by
The Crowood Press Ltd
Ramsbury, Marlborough
Wiltshire SN8 2HR

British Library Cataloguing-in-Publication Data

A catalogue record for this book is available from the British Library.

ISBN 1 85223 740 6

Picture credits

All photographs by the author.

Line-drawings by Claire Upsdale-Jones.

Typeset by Footnote Graphics, Warminster, Wiltshire
Printed and bound in Great Britain by
BPCC Hazell Books Ltd

CONTENTS

INTRODUCTION

Pine furniture has become very popular in recent years, although there is nothing new about using softwood to make tables, chairs and cabinets. Pine has the advantage of being a relatively inexpensive material to purchase, and it is always most satisfying to fill your home with furniture that you have made yourself.

The projects that appear in this book cover a wide range of items, some of which seem to have an enduring appeal on account of their basic simplicity; but they all share one thing in common: however difficult or complicated they may seem, each piece of furniture is quite straightforward and logical in design.

Wherever possible, the woodworking joints are kept to those most commonly known, and you will not be expected to have experience of any of the more elaborate or obscure varieties. Certainly you will require a reasonably wide selection of tools, including a jig-saw and router, if you are to obtain first-class results.

Inevitably, some of the projects involve a certain amount of wood-turning to produce chair and table legs. It is worth bearing in mind that small workbench-mounted lathes are not necessarily much more costly than two or three ordinary power tools, and with a little practice you will be surprised and pleased at the results that can be achieved.

The items in this book are presented mainly in order of difficulty and the amount of material that is needed to make them, which is a reflection of their cost. However, one of the most rewarding aspects of building some of the larger pieces of furniture is that you will save a lot of money by making them yourself rather than buying them ready-made in a furniture store – and of course they will be unique in the sense that you have put your own effort and interpretation into them.

Before commencing with the projects, let us first of all consider the material that we are proposing to use, the tools that will most often be required, the types of glue most suited to the task of joining the wood together, and the various finishes that may finally be applied to the surfaces of the wood.

TOOLS AND MATERIALS

Furniture made from pinewood is characterized by having plenty of knots, a rather prominent end-grain clearly displaying the timber's annual growth rings and, in its natural state, the wood is straw-coloured, perhaps with a tinge of reddish-yellow. The feature that most distinguishes it from other types of wood used in furniture-making is that pine is a softwood whereas most of the others are hardwood.

The term 'softwood' is used when referring to timber such as pine which comes from trees that retain their leaves, or needles, all the year; and 'hardwood' derives from deciduous trees which lose their leaves once a year. It so happens that pine is comparatively less dense than many of the hardwoods employed in the making of furniture, and indeed it is a softer material to work with, having a larger, more fibrous grain structure. However, the degree of softness or hardness of the wood ought not to be taken as having anything to do with the terms softwood and hardwood, because some softwoods are particularly dense, and some hardwoods are especially light in weight and extremely porous.

In fact, the wood used for the making of pine furniture does not necessarily come from a pine tree at all, but could be redwood, whitewood or deal. Pine has simply come to mean a light-coloured softwood which has a fair number of knots dotted along its surface. For our purposes, it is probably best to concentrate on redwood, since there should be a plentiful supply of this material in the stock of timber kept by most large wood merchants and DIY stores.

Redwood is the material commonly used in joinery, and compared with most of the hardwoods it is reasonably cheap to purchase, so that your endeavours in making pine furniture will additionally be rewarded by the knowledge that it is not costing as much as an equivalent amount of sapele, ash, beech or oak.

When you set out to buy the wood you need, remember that timber is usually supplied in two states: sawn and prepared. There is an important difference between these two conditions. If you ask for a length of *sawn* redwood measuring 50 × 25mm (2 × 1in), you will discover that its cross-sectional dimensions should measure precisely that amount, but the surface of the wood will be quite rough as it has only been sawn to size and not planed. Sawn timber is not suitable for furniture-making, but it is commonly used in carpentry and general building work when it will eventually be out of sight.

Planed timber is derived from the sawn

state, so that a length of prepared red-wood quoted as being 50 × 25mm (2 × 1in) PSE or PAR – standing for Planed Square Edge or Planed All Round – actually measures less than this, since the planing of the sides and edges has removed a small amount, so that the finished size ends up being closer to 45 × 19mm ($1\frac{3}{4}$ × $\frac{3}{4}$in).

The dimensions specified in the cutting lists are invariably finished sizes, the only exception being when you need to obtain a large block of wood to cut out a specially shaped section, in which instance it is often more economic to choose sawn wood because it is going to have to be cut out and planed anyway. But these occasions are comparatively rare, and most of the time you will be purchasing planed material.

It is already taken for granted that the surfaces of the material will be covered with knots, but this does not mean that all knotted wood is acceptable. In fact, the knot represents the point at which a branch joined the trunk of the tree, and provided it is live and quite small, it should present no real problem; but large dead knots are a liability and ought to be avoided. They are distinguished by a surrounding black mark, and are often rather loose and ready to drop out, leaving an awkward hole.

Take care in choosing lengths of wood, inspecting the knots and bearing in mind what type of furniture you are intending to make, how small or large it will be, and whether you will be cutting each length up into a number of shorter pieces, thus distributing the knots around various finished surfaces. At the same time, you must watch out for other faults: a badly warped board is not much use, except on the rarest of occasions

when the bending is required for a special purpose. The distortion is caused by uneven drying of the sap in the wood, and tensions arising inside the material. Another bad fault is known as 'shakes', which are splits or cracks running through a length of timber, rendering it useless.

Not all of the material you will need to buy is redwood or whitewood. Certain component parts, such as drawer-bottom panels, are cut from thin plywood, or you may wish to use sections of hardboard. Both of these are readily obtainable, and plywood is supplied in various thicknesses and differing qualities of finish.

HANDTOOLS

Much of your success in the realms of woodwork depends on the number of tools that you have at your disposal, their quality and the condition in which they are kept. There are, of course, a number of tools which must be regarded as absolutely essential if you are to produce top-quality results. No doubt you will already possess a few items – most of us accumulate a variety of tools over the years – but if you do need to add to the collection, make a point of buying well-known brand names that can be relied upon to have a long working life. Cheap tools are invariably a false economy.

Let us consider which tools you should aim to include in your tool cabinet.

The Pencil

Always keep one or two pencils available on the workbench, each with a sharp point. Avoid using a pencil with a hard lead, because this will score the soft surface of the wood and the marks could prove extremely difficult to remove later at the sandpapering stage. Nor do you want a very soft lead, as this rapidly loses its fine point, resulting in thick lines. An HB lead is a good compromise.

The Tape Measure

All woodworking depends for its success on accurate measurement, and the rule or tape measure is probably used more than any other single tool. The spring-loaded flexible steel tape measure pulls out from a metal casing, has a lock to hold it in any position and retracts back into the casing when not in use. The scale is marked on one face in centimetres and inches, with an L-shaped steel lip serving to mark the zero position, hooking easily over the end or the edge of the wood to facilitate quick measuring.

The Pair of Compasses

As there are many occasions when you will need to mark complete circles or sections of a circle accurately on the surface of a piece of wood, you should include a pair of geometrical compasses in the tool cabinet. Sometimes you need to describe a particularly large circle whose radius exceeds that of the small drawing instrument. With a little ingenuity, you can easily hinge two lengths of wood together at one end with a nut-and-bolt arrangement, and fasten a panel pin and a pencil at the opposite free ends.

The Marking Knife

Although this is normally used when the marking calls for a thin line to be scribed on the surface of the wood, the marking knife may also usefully be employed to cut right through thin pieces of material, such as plywood, in preference to using a saw. In the preparing of joints, and as a preliminary to cutting with the tenon saw, it is good practice to score along the marked pencil lines using the knife and the square, or some other form of straight edge, as there will be less tendency for the saw-blade to lift away the grain from the cut edge or end-grain.

The Square

When marking out wood in readiness for cutting, it is usual practice to draw a line at right-angles to its length. The square consists of a rectangular wooden handle, edged in brass, which has a steel blade attached to it at 90 degrees with two parallel edges.

The Marking Gauge

This tool, used for scribing a single line along a piece of wood, has a wooden stock in which a hardened steel spur is mounted at one end, and a sliding wooden fence that can be locked in any position. Strictly speaking, the marking gauge is designed to mark lines that run in the same direction as the wood grain. For marking across the grain, a slightly different tool called a cutting gauge is used, which has a sharp steel blade instead of a spur, to cut through the fibres of the wood without tearing or snatching. However, with care the marking gauge can be used for both purposes.

The Mortise Gauge

Similar in appearance to the marking

gauge, the mortise gauge differs in that it has two spurs, one of which is adjustable, so that two parallel lines can be marked on the wood. Most mortise gauges combine two functions by having double spurs on one side of the stock to mark mortises, and a single spur on the opposite side to provide a marking facility.

The Handsaw

This is a general-purpose saw used for doing most preparatory cutting. The teeth are set in an alternating pattern so that as the saw cuts into the wood, it creates a passage known as the kerf that is wider than the thickness of the blade, thus preventing it from jamming within the wood as the saw progresses through its cut.

The Tenon Saw

As its name suggests, the tenon saw is mostly used for cutting tenons and other types of joint. It is shorter than the handsaw, and the top edge of the blade is strengthened with a steel or brass back to give rigidity and ensure a straight cut. The teeth are finer than those of the handsaw, and set closer together to give a more refined cut.

The Coping Saw

A very useful saw when you need to cut curves, its thin blade is mounted in a metal frame shaped in the form of a U, and held under tension by tightening the handgrip. If the handgrip is slackened off, the blade can be rotated about its axis within the frame to set it at any desired angle. As the blade can be removed from the frame, the coping saw can be used to

cut internal holes within the wood by firstly drilling through the piece with the brace and bit, inserting the free end of the blade, and re-attaching it to the frame before commencing the cut.

The Hacksaw

The hacksaw bears a close resemblance to the coping saw, because the blade is held in a metal frame and can be changed when the teeth wear down. The chief differences are that the teeth are much finer and the blade cannot be rotated. The hacksaw is mostly used for cutting metal, but it is equally useful for sawing hardwood dowelling or similar material, when the fineness of the blade makes for a smooth, light cut.

The Chisel

It is desirable to have a good set of chisels covering a range of sizes so that you can select the most suitable width of blade for the job in hand. Typical blade widths are 6mm ($\frac{1}{4}$in), 9mm ($\frac{3}{8}$in), 13mm ($\frac{1}{2}$in), 16mm ($\frac{5}{8}$in), 19mm ($\frac{3}{4}$in), 22mm ($\frac{7}{8}$in) and 25mm (1in), although it is not necessary to include all of these sizes in your own tool outfit. There are various types of chisel, and each has its own particular characteristics. For instance, the firmer chisel has a strong cutting blade with square edges, and is used for cutting mortises and similar joints; the bevelled chisel, in which two edges of the blade are sloped, is ideal for cutting dovetail joints, or for any other sort of work where an adjacent edge of wood forms less than 90 degrees; and the mortise chisel has a thickened blade which resists any tendency to bend when cutting large deep mortises, where great pressure is exerted. For making pine furniture, where the rather soft, fibrous wood is quite easy to cut, the bevelled chisel is the best choice. The cutting edge of the blade must always be kept perfectly sharp.

The Smoothing Plane

This is the most frequently used bench plane, and is employed for planing down sawn edges of wood and preparing chamfers and bevels. However, it will only work efficiently if the blade is sharpened at frequent intervals.

The Spokeshave

The purpose of the spokeshave is mainly to shape curved surfaces that have already been cut with the coping saw or jig-saw, but which would be impossible to smooth down with the flat smoothing plane. The spokeshave can be put to other uses, including the preparing of chamfers and bevels in short lengths of wood.

The Plough Plane

Known also as the combination plane, this useful tool consists of a cast-iron body to which the blade is attached, together with the handle. Two parallel steel rods protrude sideways from the body of the plane and carry the adjustable cast-iron fence. There is a depth guide which can be raised or lowered to suit the requirements of the cut. A range of cutters can be fitted to the plough plane, providing a variety of operations: grooving, filleting, reeding, rebating and preparing edge mouldings.

The Brace Drill

This tool is used for the majority of drilling operations. It consists of a crank forged from steel that is fitted with a rounded wooden or plastic handle at one end and a chuck at the other, for holding a variety of drill bits.

The Hand Drill

A more compact type of drill than the brace, the hand drill does not have a crank, but the motive power is supplied by turning a wheel that is set midway along the frame and geared to two pinions that turn the chuck. The drilling action is firm and positive, but does not provide the same torque, or turning effect, as the brace. The hand drill is ideally suited to light drilling work, and for getting into restricted corners where it would be impossible to turn the crank of the brace.

Drill Bits

These provide the drill with its cutting edge. Those used in the brace are square-tanged so that they can be gripped by the chuck, but power drills usually only accept bits that have round shanks. The hand drill, depending on the type of chuck fitted, will take either one or the other.

For drilling very small diameter holes in wood or plywood, the twist drill is best. Medium-sized holes, ranging from 6mm ($\frac{1}{4}$in) to 13mm ($\frac{1}{2}$in) in diameter, should be drilled with long spiral-shaped auger bits, particularly for boring a straight hole deep into end-grain, as in the preparing of dowel joints; whereas for larger-diameter holes, the choice is normally the centre bit, which resembles the cutting tip of the auger bit but does not have a long spiral shaft.

The Wooden Mallet

The mallet is used whenever a blow needs to be struck in the course of cutting joints and assembling the work – with the exception of driving in nails and panel pins. The mallet's large head is usually made of beech, and the handle, which is wedge-shaped to prevent the head from flying off, is often cut from ash. Both materials are very hard and durable.

POWER TOOLS

The Electric Jig-Saw

In its most common form, this is a hand-held power tool in which the saw blade oscillates up and down at very high speed to provide a fast and highly manoeuvrable means of cutting. Some of the more expensive models have a range of speed settings, and a knob may be provided to turn the blade. There are many occasions when the jig-saw is an invaluable tool, especially for cutting around curved lines.

The Electric Router

This is probably the most specialized tool that the woodworker is likely to buy, with the possible exception of a lathe, and it is well worth setting enough money aside to purchase a good one. There is always an element of mystery about a tool that has a reputation for performing many functions, in this case

rebating, edge-moulding, grooving and fluting, to name but a few. In fact, the electric router is simply a motor housed vertically inside the body of the tool, which drives the chuck at very high revolutions. Into the chuck may be fitted a wide range of cutters. Because the cutter turns at such a high speed, it produces a very clean cut regardless of whether the router is moved along in the same direction as the grain or at right-angles to it, making this tool more versatile than the plough plane. The base of the router is circular, so that it can be lined up beside a length of straight-edged batten, acting as its guide, and steered at any angle without deviating from a straight path. A detachable fence can be mounted beneath the base to provide the router with its own adjustable guide – or a special plate enables it to cut in a circle – and the spring-loaded plunging action of the body can be pre-set against a scaled depth stop so that the cutter is accurately controlled both laterally and vertically.

The Lathe

As several of the projects in this book involve wood-turning, you are faced with the choice of either hiring or borrowing the services of a full-sized cabinet-type lathe from a local joinery or workshop, or purchasing a smaller and simpler version which can be attached to your own workbench. The latter course of action is undoubtedly preferable, because although miniature lathes do not have the same capacity or potential as their larger counterparts, it is nevertheless possible to achieve excellent results with them. As a matter of interest, the wood-turning illustrated in the examples in this book is carried out on a lathe attachment for an electric drill. The bed of the lathe is securely fastened at the back of the workbench, a two-speed drill is mounted in a special frame at one end, to which the headstock is attached, and the tailstock is fastened to a metal casting which is able to slide up and down on the bed, and is capable of being locked in any position. An adjustable tool-rest occupies the space in between, and likewise this can be secured tightly in any required position.

The only disadvantage with this arrangement is that there is a limit to the length of material that can be turned – all lathes have their limits, but this is rather restricted in the electric drill lathe attachment – but its range has been extended by fastening the casting of the tailstock to a separate block of wood which is screwed firmly to the workbench in very accurate alignment with the lathe bed.

You will also require a set of special wood-turning tools, comprising a spindle gouge, parting tool and chisel which can usually be purchased as a set, and perhaps one or two additional narrow gouges for shaping small curves.

Even if you have no previous experience of wood-turning, you will find that it is well worth devoting some time and money to equipping your own workshop with a lathe facility, practising on a few pieces of scrap wood to get the feel of manipulating the various tools and then attempting one of the wood-turning projects. Producing a range of turned components for tables, chairs and cabinets is most enjoyable and satisfying, extending your scope for making fine good-quality furniture.

SAFETY PRECAUTIONS

Accidents usually happen very quickly and can be avoided by taking care at all times. Tools such as the saw and the chisel must always be kept sharp if they are to be effective in cutting the wood, but this means that they will be devastatingly effective in cutting fingers that happen to get in the way. When you have to hold the workpiece with your free hand, keep it well out of the saw's reach, and behind the blade of the chisel.

Always take adequate precautions when using power tools, such as the wearing of protective goggles to cover your eyes, a face mask to avoid inhaling fine dust particles and ear-muffs to safeguard your hearing from the loud whine of an electric router or jig-saw, or indeed the lathe. Switch off power tools when they are not in use, isolating their plugs from the power supply. Never let wood shavings or sawdust accumulate on the workbench or the surrounding floor, because they are a potential fire risk as well as a menace for slipping on.

GLUES AND FIXINGS

The strength of a good wood glue lies in its ability to spread in liquid form across the full extent of the joining surfaces, covering a relatively large area. If you could examine the surface of the wood in microscopic detail, you would discover that no matter how smooth it appears to the naked eye or feels to the touch, it is, in fact, totally irregular and full of tiny cavities. The glue, possessing the capacity to flow, searches out these holes or crevices and fills them. As it begins to set, the internal molecular structure of the glue locks into a chain and eventually becomes a single solid mass, often stronger than the wood itself.

The conditions necessary for a successful bond are that the two joining surfaces be clean, dry and free from traces of oil or grease. Once the glue has been applied to both parts of the joint, it is assembled and clamped firmly together for the prescribed period of time while the glue sets hard.

There are several different types of glue available for joining wood together, but the one preferred by the author and used in all of the projects in this book is the urea formaldehyde powdered resin variety, to which a measured quantity of cold water must be added and stirred in thoroughly, making an active and workable mixture that is ready for use within a matter of seconds.

An old cup will serve as a suitable mixing vessel and an old spoon as a means of measuring out the powder and the water. To apply the glue, use a clean flexible paintbrush: a large decorating-type brush for the bigger joints and more extensive joining areas, or a small cheap artist's brush for narrow grooves and tiny joints. Temperature does not play a critical role in the use of this glue as it does with Scotch glue, but an ambient temperature of at least 15°C (59°) is desirable.

When a glued joint needs to be strengthened, dowel pegs are often employed to reinforce what would otherwise be plain abutting surfaces, and these can be cut to the required length from various diameters of hardwood dowelling material, or countersunk mild steel woodscrews may be used instead. These are supplied in different gauges and lengths. Screws are particularly useful for assembling joints in the absence of glue, in which case it is always possible to dismantle the joints easily afterwards.

An alternative method is to secure a joint with a nut-and-bolt arrangement: this is not necessarily any stronger than an equivalent size of woodscrew, but it can be put together and taken apart again more frequently without causing undue wear and tear to the wood.

WOOD FINISHES

How do you decide what is the best finish for a particular piece of furniture? Is polyurethane varnish better than French polish, or should the piece be brushed with a glaze or rubbed with an oil or a wax polish? In the end, the choice is mainly a matter of personal preference, added to the more practical considerations such as the type and size of furniture and to what use it will be put. If your pine furniture is going to be subjected to a great deal of use, generally knocked about, and with food and drink occasionally spilled over it, simply applying several coats of modern varnish has a lot to recommend it.

Varnishes

Old-fashioned varnishes were made by dissolving gums and resins in linseed oil, alcohol or water, and were rather slow to dry. By comparison, the modern synthetic polyurethane range of varnishes are easy to apply by brush, dry fairly quickly, are not so much affected by the surrounding air temperature and give a tough, heat-resisting and waterproof finish which is ideal for furniture in daily use.

Polyurethane varnishes come in three different types, drying to a gloss, satin or matt finish. The same manufacturers also supply a range of coloured varnishes so that you can, up to a point, use them in place of wood dye – not that this really applies in the making of pine furniture, which is rarely stained. If there is a fault with synthetic varnishes, it is the inherent lack of adhesion and penetration into the grain, though this is being steadily improved in successive formulas.

Varnishes are applied with a soft, fine-bristled brush, and you may need as many as four coats before a really satisfactory finish is achieved. Each coat is allowed to dry completely, and then rubbed down with wire wool or very fine sandpaper before commencing the next coat. The brushwork must be carried out carefully to avoid creating tiny air bubbles which eventually dry to form craters, and to even out the brush strokes so that the varnish spreads over the surface in a uniformly smooth covering.

Varnish applied by spray-gun would achieve an extremely fine quality finish.

Oils

At one time, the term 'oil' normally referred to the substance known as linseed oil, and was widely used in the treatment of wood to afford it protection and add a shine to the surface. Linseed oil soaks into the wood and gives a good heat-resisting finish, but its main disadvantage is that it takes a long time to dry – as anyone who has used it to oil a cricket-bat will know!

Teak oil and Danish oil have become very popular. Though both types are referred to collectively, there is a small difference between them. They each have the property of priming, sealing and finishing the wood to leave a soft, lustrous appearance.

Polishes

Wax polish can be applied directly to the wood, either in liquid or cake form, and is perhaps the most satisfactory way of finishing wood, as it can so easily be re-applied at any time. Wax polish is applied to the wood using a soft lint-free cloth and must be rubbed well into the grain. It cannot be too strongly emphasized that the more effort that is put into the rubbing action, the better the shine. Some polishes are specially blended for light woods like pine, while others have a deeper tone.

French polish creates a much more refined appearance than any other type of wood treatment, resulting in an almost glass-like surface with a high reflectiveness. The drawback is that it demands great skill in its application, and is not suited to everyday use, so considerable care must be taken to protect those pieces of furniture to which it has been applied.

CHAPTER ONE

BOOKCASE SHELVING UNIT

The bookcase can be used as a free-standing piece of furniture, or it may be fastened to the wall with screws and re-garded as a shelf unit for displaying ornaments. Its versatility arises from the fact that it is designed with a deep base to give stability when it stands on its own, and has two battens built in at the back, one on each side, through which screws can be driven to fasten it in position on any flat wall. The bookcase is very simple in construction, consisting of two end panels, into which four shelves are fitted with housing joints, and the two battens are notched in to the rear edge of each shelf. The end panels become progressively wider from the top to bottom, in accordance with which the four shelves increase in width. A decorative pattern is given to the front edge of the two end panels.

Begin by cutting out the end panels from two pieces of material each measuring 915mm (36in) in length, 222mm (8¾in) in width and 19mm (¾in) thick. Lay the two pieces level with each other on the workbench, edge to edge, and mark in simultaneously the four shelf positions and the width of the end panels at these points. For guidance, measuring from the top end of the panels and working

Cutting List
End panel: two of 915 × 222 × 19mm (36 × 8¾ × ¾in)
Top shelf: one of 890 × 143 × 19mm (35 × 5⅝ × ¾in)
Second shelf: one of 890 × 168 × 19mm (35 × 6⅝ × ¾in)
Third shelf: one of 890 × 194 × 19mm (35 × 7⅝ × ¾in)
Bottom shelf: one of 890 × 222 × 19mm (35 × 8¾ × ¾in)
Batten: two of 762 × 45 × 19mm (30 × 1¾ × ¾in)

downwards: the top shelf measures 143mm (5⅝in) wide and is set down 146mm (5¾in) from the end-grain to its upper surface: the second shelf measures 168mm (6⅝in) wide and is set down by 368mm (14½in); the third shelf measures 194mm (7⅝in) wide and is set down by 616mm (24¼in); and the bottom shelf measures 222mm (8¾in) wide, and its position is set up by 13mm (½in) from the end-grain at the bottom of the end panels to its under surface. In between each shelf level is a curved bracket-shaped decoration which leaves a flat portion in the area of the shelves measuring 55mm (2⅛in) in length.

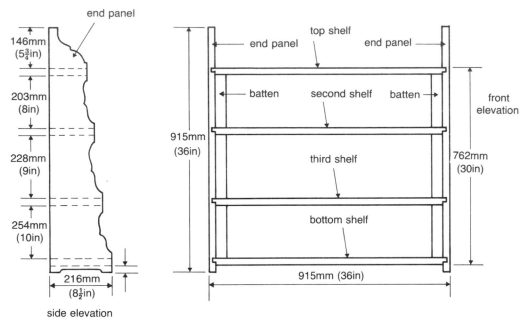

Main dimensions of the bookcase shelving unit.

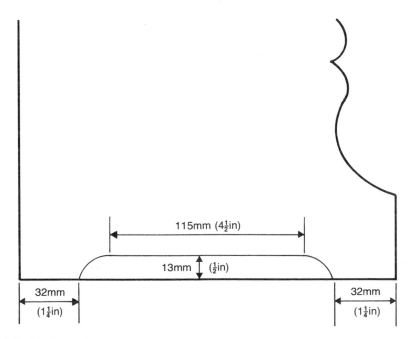

Dimensions of the bookcase base.

Mark the curved 'bracket'-shaped lines freehand on the end panel.

Once the shelf positions and the short flat portions of the front edge have been established on both of the end panels, the curved 'bracket' lines may either be drawn in freehand – in which case there could be a slight discrepancy between the two – or you could mark out and cut three separate card templates and use these to guarantee accuracy. At the top of each end panel, two quarter-circles are drawn in with a pair of geometrical compasses, with a narrow step between them, the uppermost curve being set 25mm (1in) from the rear edge. At the bottom of the end panels, two feet are formed by measuring shallow curves 32mm (1¼in) from each edge and joining up with a straight line, parallel to the end-grain, positioned in such a way as to be flush with the bottom surface of the lowest shelf.

It may be argued that the surest way of maintaining accuracy between the two end panels is to clamp them together in perfect alignment, and cut them both to shape at once with the electric jig-saw, and indeed this method will probably prove entirely successful. However, it does have one drawback: in doubling

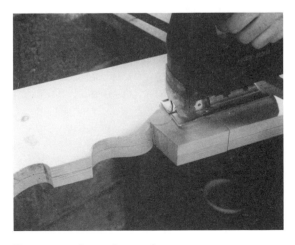

The two end panels may be cut out simultaneously with the jig-saw, taking care to keep the blade working a square edge.

Complete the shaping of the curves with the spokeshave.

the thickness of wood that must be cut, you increase resistance to the passage of the jig-saw blade, and the decorative 'bracket' shapes contain rather sharp curves which make it possible to bend the saw blade slightly. If this were to happen, one set of curves would be cut more deeply than the other. It is preferable, therefore, to cut the curves in the two panels separately, for at least any small errors will now be consistent.

After cutting out, the curves may require some attention with the spokeshave and a wide-bladed chisel before they appear entirely satisfactory, and the stepped flat front edges should be planed level with the smoothing plane.

The next step is to measure and mark in the housing joint grooves for the four shelf panels on the inside face of each end panel. On this occasion it is certainly more advisable to mark in the groove positions on one panel, and cut them out, before transferring their positions on to the second panel, as this gives a greater assurance that the four shelves will fit perfectly and not tend to pull the assembly out of its true alignment. Each

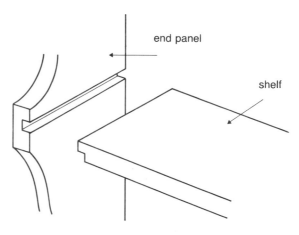

end panel

shelf

The housing joint.

Mark in the housing joint grooves on the inside face of the two end panels with the square and pencil.

Scribe in the depth of each housing groove with the marking gauge.

groove should be marked to a width of 9mm (⅜in) and a depth of 6mm (¼in), using a square to pencil two parallel lines across the wood, and a marking gauge to scribe depth lines on both edges.

The grooves may be cut by one of two methods. The first of these is to clamp the end panel firmly to the workbench, with the groove markings facing uppermost, and score along the squared pencil lines with a sharp knife. Taking the tenon saw, cut down on the waste side of both groove lines as far as the scribed depth lines, and then gradually chop out the waste from the groove using a 9mm (⅜in) chisel and mallet, working the chisel firstly from one end and then from the other. Take care to ensure that the depth of the groove is consistent throughout its entire length: if not enough waste is re-

Cut along the squared pencil lines with the tenon saw, cutting down to the gauged depth lines.

Remove the waste from the housing grooves by chopping away all of the unwanted wood with the chisel and mallet.

The edge of the shelf is planed down until it measures the required width.

moved from the middle area, the shelf will not fit fully.

The second method of preparing the grooves is to use an electric router, fitted with a 9mm (⅜in) diameter straight cutter. Adjust the depth guide on the router so that it cuts to a maximum depth of 6mm (¼in), and then clamp a straight-edged piece of wood across the end panel in such a position that it serves to steer the router accurately across the width of the piece in exactly the right place, having already aligned the blade of the cutter with the marked groove. Once everything has been set up and double-checked, the router will cut a perfect groove in just a single run, and in this instance a consistent depth is assured.

When all eight of the grooves have been cut satisfactorily, the next step is to mark and cut the tongues at the ends of

the four shelves. The shelves should already have been cut to length, and their edges planed as necessary so that they are equal to the width of the end panels at the point where they are to be fitted. Obviously, all of the shelves must be of the same length, otherwise the finished bookcase will be lopsided.

Having cut and planed the ends square, set the marking gauge to a gap of 9mm (⅜in) and scribe a line across each end-grain, and at the end of each edge. Then square in a line 6mm (¼in) from the end so that it is marked across the width of the shelf on its underside, and mark also on the two edges so that the pencil line meets the scribed gauge line.

Once again, score along the pencilled line with a sharp knife, clamp the shelf securely to the top of the workbench, and remove the waste with the tenon saw, cutting down on the waste side of the scored line; then place the wood up-

Scribe a line across the width of the shelf
on the underside with the marking gauge.

After sawing down the scribed lines, use
the chisel to ease off the waste if it fails to
come away by hand.

right in the vice and saw on the waste
side of the scribed line until the unwanted portion drops away. Clean up
the surfaces of the tongue with the
chisel, and make a test fitting in its
groove. It is better to make the tongue
slightly too large, and have to trim away
a little more wood with the chisel, than to
have a loose fit.

When all of the tongues have been
prepared, make a trial assembly of the
bookcase to see that all of the joints fit
together.

Now for the fitting of the two battens.
These are important because they not
only provide the means of screwing the
bookcase to the wall, but they also give
the structure its rigidity. Without them,
the bookcase could easily have a tendency
to lean one way or the other during
assembly, but the addition of the battens
ensures that the shelves meet the end
panels at right-angles.

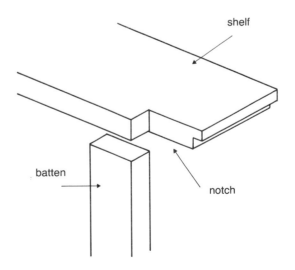

The batten fits into the notch on
the shelf.

Cut away the waste with the tenon saw to create the notches for the battens.

Cut the two battens to length from material measuring 45 × 19mm (1¾ × ¾in), their correct length simply being the distance from the upper surface of the top shelf to the lower surface of the bottom shelf. Make sure that their ends are marked and cut perfectly square.

Mark in the notches to receive the battens at both ends of each shelf. These should be 45mm (1¾in) long from the shoulder of the tongue, and 19mm (¾in) deep from the rear edge, the lines being marked in with the square, pencil and marking gauge. The battens must fit as tightly as possible, so when you cut out the notches make sure that the blade of the tenon saw works just to the waste side of the marked lines, holding the material securely in the vice as the saw is manipulated.

Make a second trial assembly of the bookcase, this time to check that the two battens can be fitted in place without disturbing the security of the tongues in their grooves.

Mix a large quantity of wood glue, and apply it by brush to all of the grooves, the inside surfaces of the tongues, and to the edges of the notches in the shelves. Fit the shelves to the end panels, and tap the battens into place so that their square-cut upper ends lie flush with the upper surface of the top shelf. The assembly is rather large for cramps to be fitted, and the best alternative is to set the bookcase on one side and place heavy weights on it in the form of bricks or blocks, standing these on old newspapers to prevent the surface of the wood from being scratched.

If you intend standing the bookcase on the floor, it is not necessary to do anything further except to rub it down with sandpaper and apply a suitable finish to the wood. But if the bookcase is to be attached to a wall in the form of fitted shelves, drill four screw-holes in the battens, two on each side, and countersink the holes, using a hand-drill fitted firstly with a No. 10 drill and then a rose-head countersink.

PICNIC TABLE

The folding picnic table is a useful item for the household or the garden, and its design and method of construction are quite simple and straightforward, as it makes use of the most basic of woodworking joints, the abutting lapped joint. The table top consists of ten slats, regularly spaced, and mounted upon two long rails which form the frame of the table. Gaps between the slats give the table its characteristic appearance, and have a practical purpose when used out of doors by allowing rain water or spilt drinks to drain away without soaking the entire table top. Two hinged pairs of legs are attached to the frame, and can either be folded completely flat when the table is not in use so that it is more convenient to carry around and takes up less room to store, or they can be opened out into a rigid criss-cross structure, the free leg locking into place beneath the frame. The table stands 640mm (25$\frac{3}{16}$in) high, and the top measures 810 × 610mm (31$\frac{7}{8}$ × 24in).

The first step is to measure and cut the ten slats for the table top equally to length, noting that all of the slats are rounded at each end. These semi-circular curves are marked in with a pair of geometrical compasses, setting the radius to half the width of the wood – the width being 70mm (2$\frac{3}{4}$in), and the required radius 35mm (1$\frac{3}{8}$in). The overall

Cutting List	
Table top slat:	ten of 610 × 70 × 19mm (24 × 2$\frac{3}{4}$ × $\frac{3}{4}$in)
Table rail:	two of 810 × 45 × 19mm (31$\frac{7}{8}$ × 1$\frac{3}{4}$ × $\frac{3}{4}$in)
Leg:	four of 863 × 45 × 19mm (34 × 1$\frac{3}{4}$ × $\frac{3}{4}$in)
Outer crossbar:	two of 492 × 45 × 19mm (19$\frac{3}{4}$ × 1$\frac{3}{4}$ × $\frac{3}{4}$in)
Inner crossbar:	one of 448 × 45 × 19mm (17$\frac{5}{8}$ × 1$\frac{3}{4}$ × $\frac{3}{4}$in)

length of each slat having been marked with a square and pencil, measure a second line 35mm (1$\frac{3}{8}$in) in from both ends, squaring in very faintly with the pencil, to provide a line upon which to place the point of the compasses halfway across the width of the material. Draw in the semi-circular curve.

Clamp the wood horizontally in the vice and remove the curved portions of waste with a coping saw or hacksaw. An electric jig-saw will speed up the work of cutting, but you may find that performing this task by hand permits a greater degree of accuracy, especially as the curves are rather tight.

Next, measure and mark the two table rails to length, allowing a small amount of waste at each end – which will later be

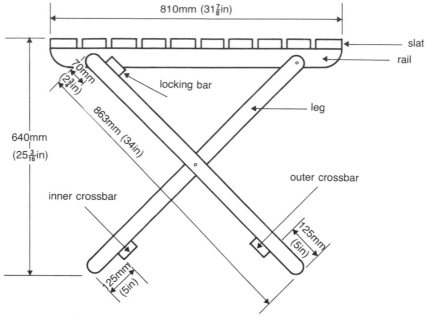

Main dimensions of the table.

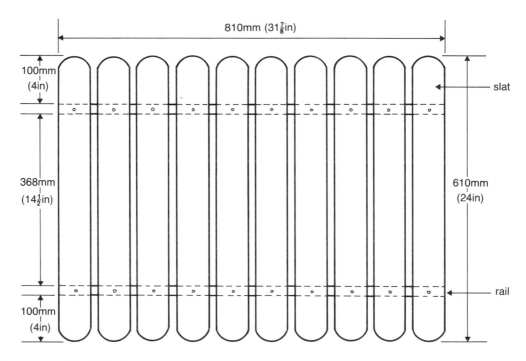

Dimensions of the table top.

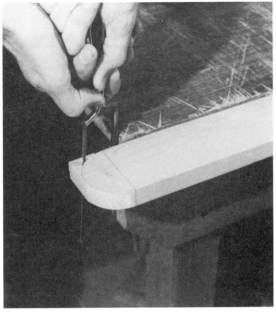

Draw a semi-circular curve at the end of each slat, using a pair of geometrical compasses.

Cut the curved ends to shape using a hacksaw, coping saw or jig-saw.

trimmed away – and mark in a quadrant curve at both ends, setting the radius of the compasses this time to a distance equal to the 70mm (2¾in) width of the material.

The slats are mounted on the top edges of the two rails in such a way that they lie at right-angles and form simple lapped joints, in which the adjoining surfaces abut, and are held firmly in place by gluing and screwing them together. It could be argued that greater strength would be achieved by notching the top edges of the two rails to a depth of 6mm (¼in) or so, thereby seating the slats more accurately with less tendency to slip out of the perpendicular. Indeed, there is no reason why you should not proceed with the preparation of notches if you wish to strengthen the laps, but for this type of

table they are not considered really necessary.

Each rail is set in by 100mm (4in) from the rounded ends of the slats, and the screw-holes in the slats are positioned so that the screws pass centrally into the rails. Since the rails are 19mm (¾in) thick, the centre of each screw-hole should be 109mm (4⅜in) from the end of the slat, and placed halfway across its width. One tip before you begin drilling the screw-holes in the slats: experience of using the handbrace and its accompanying drill-bit demonstrates that no matter how much care you take to hold the brace vertically and square with respect to the surface of the wood, it is possible for the bit to wander very slightly as it cuts through the material, and emerge on the opposite side in a marginally different place. This effect may be counteracted by squaring

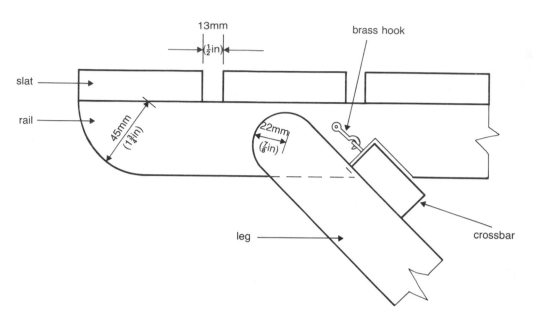

Side view of the table.

all around the wood, and marking the centre of the hole on each of the opposite surfaces, and drilling from both sides so that the hole meets in the middle, thus ensuring accuracy. This method is recommended here, so that there is precision and consistency in the positioning of the holes.

Drill the holes through the slats using a No. 8 bit mounted in the handbrace, and countersink each hole on the upper surface of the slat so that the heads of the screws lie flush with the material.

Now arrange the slats on the rails in their exact positions – the slats are spaced approximately 13mm ($\frac{1}{2}$in) apart, and may require a certain amount of adjustment before you are satisfied that all of the gaps are the same – checking that the two end slats each lie up against the marked quadrant curves on the rails. When all

seems well, pass a bradawl through each screw-hole so that the pointed tip pierces a mark on the top edge of the rail beneath. Before dismantling, lightly pencil a number on each slat to identify the order, 1 to 10. Do the same for the rails,

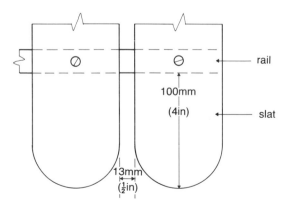

Construction of the slats.

Position the slats on the rails and mark the screw holes. Lightly screw the slats in place to check the spacing.

so that you know which one is which. This will permit all the components to be fitted together with great accuracy, instead of preparing the holes in the rails, picking up the slats at random and hoping that the holes match up. This is also the time to mark the positions of the slats on the rails if you intend marking and cutting notches in the top edges of the rails.

Clamp each rail securely in the vice and drill into the ten marked indentations along the top edge using the same No. 8 drill bit, boring to a depth of 25mm (1in). In spite of all the care already taken, it is still a good idea to assemble the slats temporarily on the rails, using twenty 50mm (2in) No. 8 woodscrews, in order to check that the spacings are correct, then dismantle and cut the ends of the rails to the marked quadrant shape with the coping saw or hacksaw.

Measure and mark the four legs to length, and draw a semi-circular curve at the ends of each one with the pair of compasses, using the same method as previously, and remove the waste.

Cut the three leg crossbars to length from wood of the same cross-section, noting that two of these are for the outer pair of legs and should measure 492mm (19¾in) in length, the other one being for the inner pair and measuring 448mm (17⅝in) in length. The two lower crossbars are located 125mm (5in) up from the bottom of the legs, and the one upper, or

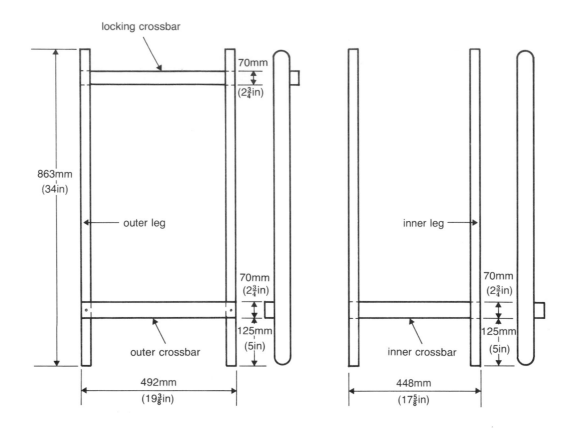

Main dimensions of the inner and outer leg assemblies.

locking, crossbar is placed 70mm (2¾in) down from the top of the outer pair, its purpose being to slot into two notches cut in the rails, thus holding the legs in their open criss-cross position.

The three crossbars are lap-jointed to the legs, using the same method as that employed for joining the slats to the rails, although the laps may be strengthened by cutting notches in the legs.

Both pairs of legs are hinged together at their centres, using 6mm (¼in) diameter bolts, and the inner pair is similarly hinged to the table rails. The hinge holes at the top of the inner pair of legs are located 22mm (⅞in) from the ends, and the corres-

ponding two holes in the rails are set 122mm (4¾in) from the end of each quadrant. All the holes are positioned centrally across the width of the wood.

As was the case when preparing the screw-holes in the slats, the bolt holes must be made with great precision, otherwise the legs might not align properly with the table rails, or with each other. Every hole position should, therefore, be measured and marked on both sides of the material, and drilled from both directions to ensure accuracy. Having marked in the holes, drill them out with a 6mm (¼in) auger bit mounted in the hand-brace, following the above procedure.

Drill the holes for the hinge bolts with a 6mm ($\frac{1}{4}$in) diameter auger bit mounted in the handbrace.

Where necessary, enlarge the reverse side of the bolt hole with a 16mm ($\frac{5}{8}$in) diameter centre bit, to recess the nut.

However, where the hinge nuts are recessed into the wood – on the inside edges of the inner pair (at the centre point) and on the insides of the rails – make this recess by completing the drilling with a larger 16mm ($\frac{5}{8}$in) diameter centre bit, equal in depth to the combined thickness of the nut and washer employed in the hinge arrangement.

When all the holes have been drilled, mark in the positions of the two notches for the top crossbar at the opposite end of the rails from the hinges. To find this position, and, more particularly, to determine the angle at which each notch must be cut, simply take one inner leg, one outer leg and one corresponding rail, and temporarily hinge the two legs at their centres and the inner leg to the rail,

using the nuts and bolts that will be used in the final assembly, or possibly a satisfactory substitute. Then arrange them in the 'standing' position as if the legs were fully open, setting the free top end of the

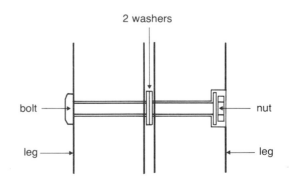

The hinge arrangement.

Cut out the notch for the locking crossbar with the hacksaw.

outer leg at the same distance from its end of the rail as the hinged leg is from the opposite end. The fact that the ends of each leg are rounded means that the folding action should not be inhibited by the table-top slats when they are fixed in place. Pencil a line against the edge of the outer leg to which the locking crossbar will be attached, which presently serves to determine the position of the notch and its angle. Complete the marking by making a rectangular card template, equal in size to the cross-sectional dimensions of the crossbar, place this on the line, and mark around it in pencil to delineate the *exact* amount of wood that must be removed. Note that the shorter side of the notch should measure 9mm (⅜in), from which the remaining proportions of the notch will automatically follow.

Clamp the two rails side by side in the vice – their alignment being critical at this point and accurately established by inserting a 6mm (¼in) diameter bolt through both hinge holes – check that their edges lie flush with one another, with the notch marking clearly visible, and cut out the waste for the two pieces simultaneously, using the coping saw or hacksaw. Begin by sawing along the two parallel lines denoting the sides of the notch, and then make a series of angled cuts within the waste area, gradually taking out more and more wood until you reach the squared end, finishing off if necessary with a narrow flat file.

All the abutting lapped joints should now be assembled, the slats of the table top being joined to the rails, and the crossbars to the legs. For each joint, apply wood glue to the two abutting sur-

Glue and screw the crossbar to each pair of legs.

faces, bring them into contact and then screw the joint tightly home, using a 50mm (2in) No. 8 woodscrew. Undoubtedly, some surplus glue will squeeze out of the joint and must be wiped away with a damp cloth. Check that the assemblies are properly square before setting them to one side for at least a day while the glue sets hard, and then rub down thoroughly with medium and fine-grade sandpaper to remove all pencil marks, smoothing out any rough areas or corners.

Select the type of finish you wish to apply to the surface of the wood, and when it has been applied and given sufficient time to dry and harden, hinge the two pairs of legs together, using two 38 × 6mm (1½ × ¼in) galvanized bolts,

The locking crossbar is engaged in the notch and secured with a small hook and eye.

washers and nuts. After tightening the nuts and checking that the legs fold and unfold as smoothly as they are intended to, without binding or rubbing, burr over the end of each bolt with a hard nail and hammer to prevent the nut from loosening.

Hinge the inner pair of legs to the rails in the same way and slot the locking crossbar into its receiver notches. Finally, attach two small brass hooks and eyes to the rails and crossbar respectively, at each side of the table, to ensure that the table cannot accidentally collapse if it is lifted and moved while the legs are in the open position.

CHAPTER THREE

STOOL

Of all the furniture that it is possible to make, the stool probably has the fewest parts and the simplest design, consisting merely of a flat seat, four straight legs and four rails linking them together. The only catch is that all of the parts need to be turned on a lathe, and this could easily deter the woodworker who has no experience of wood-turning. But, as you will see in due course, mastery of this particular craft can open up endless possibilities, and a great deal of popular pine furniture contains at least some items manufactured on a lathe.

Although lathe work often appears rather complicated, with its own special tools, as with most techniques, once you have grasped the fundamental principle and had plenty of practice, the work becomes much less arduous and you begin to experiment more and more.

The stool is a good starting point. Whether you have access to a large cabinet-type lathe with several speeds and a long bed, or a smaller, less complicated workbench-mounted lathe powered by a small electric motor of a similar capacity to a power-drill, the method is the same in either case. The larger lathe certainly offers more scope in respect of face-plate turning, as there is less restriction in the radius of wood that can be turned to produce the stool seat; how-

Cutting List	
Stool seat:	two of 280 × 147 × 32mm (11 × 5¾ × 1¼in)
Leg:	four of 676 × 45mm (26⅝ × 1¾in) diameter mopstick
Rail:	four of 242 × 32 × 32mm (9½ × 1¼ × 1¼in)

ever, lathe-turning is not the only way of preparing a circular disc of wood for this purpose.

So let us begin with the seat. Our example has a diameter of 275mm (10¹³⁄₁₆in) and a thickness of 25mm (1in). It is unlikely that you would be able to obtain a plank of wood measuring around 280mm (11in) wide, so the first task is to make up a square panel from two narrower pieces of material. Cut two lengths of pine each measuring 280mm (11in) long, 147mm (5¾in) wide and 32mm (1¼in) thick. It should be possible for your timber merchant to plane this to size from a piece of sawn timber measuring 152 × 50mm (6 × 2in).

Lay the two lengths side by side on the workbench so that two edges can be butted up against one another, in perfect contact. Although the meeting of the edges is important, due consideration must also be given to the distribution of

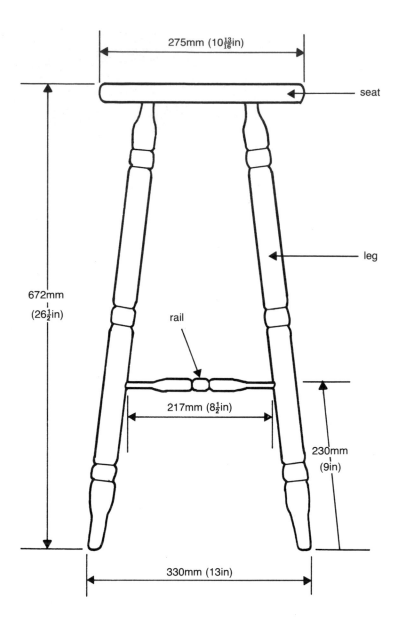

275mm (10¹³⁄₁₆in)

seat

leg

672mm
(26½in)

rail

217mm (8½in)

230mm
(9in)

330mm (13in)

Main dimensions of the stool.

knots on the two individual pieces so that when they are brought together the overall appearance seems natural, as if comprising only one piece of material.

For certain types of work it would be sufficient merely to apply a mixture of wood glue to the two abutting edges, bring them into contact under firm pressure and allow the glue to set hard, for such a joint is indeed very strong, especially when the wood is of a generous thickness. If it were your intention to mark a circle on the wood and cut out the seat disc with an electric jig-saw or router, then this would certainly be an acceptable way of joining the two pieces together.

However, if the square panel of wood is to be mounted on the face-plate of the lathe, and the seat produced by turning the material at very high speed, then it is recommended that you provide some reinforcement to the butt joint, and this should consist of three dowels set at regular intervals along the adjoining edges. The dowel joints are prepared by firstly taking a marking gauge and setting the distance between its spur and fence to half the thickness of the wood and scribing a line along both edges, working the gauge from the same side in each instance to eliminate any slight error in the exact centrality of the line.

Place the two pieces of wood side by side, with the two adjoining edges lying flush, square three pencil lines across corresponding to the positions of the dowels. These do not need to be precise with regard to where they are placed along the length of the wood, provided each pair of marked positions align.

Taking each piece of wood in turn, clamp it firmly in the vice with the scribed edge uppermost, and drill down

Scribe a line along the edge of the wood, the spur being set midway across the thickness of the piece.

into each of the three marked positions with a 9mm (⅜in) auger bit mounted in the handbrace, boring to a depth of approximately 38mm (1½in). Then cut three pieces of 9mm (⅜in) diameter dowelling to a length of 70mm (2¾in) and cut a shallow groove along the length of each with the tenon saw to provide a glue channel. Mix a small quantity of wood glue, apply it with a narrow artist's brush to the inside surface of all six holes, and to the three dowels, as well as to the abutting edges, and assemble the dowels to their holes, bringing the two pieces of wood into contact, and cramping up tightly while the glue dries and sets thoroughly.

As already indicated, there are three ways in which the circular stool seat can be cut to shape. In each case, determine the centre of the square panel by drawing

Drill three holes in the scribed edge, to receive lengths of 9mm ($\frac{3}{8}$in) diameter dowelling.

Glue the three dowels into their holes, before applying more glue to the abutting edges and assembling the two halves of the seat.

in two straight diagonal lines and, at the point where these lines intersect, place the pivot of a pair of geometrical compasses, set to a radius of 138mm ($5\frac{7}{16}$in). Scribe a circle on the surface of the wood representing the top side of the seat.

The first method of cutting out the seat circle is simply to clamp the wood at the edge of the workbench and cut carefully around the marked circular line with the jig-saw, fitted with a fine-toothed blade. Work the saw slowly and accurately, keeping the blade always just on the waste side of the line, stopping several times to release the clamps and turn the wood around so that the saw does not cut into the end of the bench. With care, this method should ensure an almost perfect circle, which can be lightly planed with the spokeshave and then sandpapered to produce an acceptable finish.

The second method is to employ the electric router, fitted with a straight-edged cutter, and an accessory which permits the router to be rotated about a central point. Fasten this accessory plate to the centre of the circle with a panel pin, and align the cutter with the outside of the circular pencil line so that it effectively cuts a deep groove *around* the circumference of the seat. In order to prevent the cutter from overheating, it is advisable to make several circuits with the router, increasing the depth of the cut each time until the waste drops away from the perimeter, leaving a clean edge which only requires sandpapering.

Remember that in either of the foregoing methods, the two halves of the stool seat could be butted together with wood glue.

The third method, undoubtedly the best for producing a high-quality finish,

Mark in the diameter of the seat with a pair of geometrical compasses.

The square seat panel is fastened to the face-plate of the lathe, with a smaller intermediate wooden block mounted in between.

is to mount the square panel to the face-plate of the lathe and turn the seat. In this example, the material must be fastened to the face-plate with four stout screws, and clearly it is not desirable to end up with a stool seat which has four gaping screw-holes in its underside, even if they are out of sight. The solution is to fix a second, smaller, square block to the surface that will eventually be the underside of the seat. Instead of gluing this other block directly to the seat – which would cause problems when it came to remove it afterwards – a thin piece of card is sandwiched in between, wood glue being applied to both sides. This provides a readily removable interface between the second block and the panel. After the glue has dried, it is the second block which is fastened to the face-plate, and the entire assembly attached to the lathe.

With such a heavy block of wood revolving at very high speed, you must safeguard yourself from injury should the interface fail, causing the seat to fly off. Protect your eyes with tough goggles and your head and body with thickly padded clothing, adding ear-muffs to deaden the continuous high-pitched whine of the machinery. Having adequately marked in the circumference of the seat so that its centre coincides with the centre of rotation of the face-plate, set the lathe turning, and apply the pointed parting tool to a position on the seat's surface just outside the circumference, and gradually remove the waste.

Turning the stool seat.

Once the circular seat has been roughed out and all the waste removed, trim the curved edge with the spindle gouge to produce rounded corners, and a straight-edged chisel to smooth the circumference. The thickness of the seat measuring approximately 32mm (1¼in), this may either be left as it is or the thickness could be reduced somewhat by applying the tip of the chisel or the parting tool to the revolving face, working from the centre outwards.

Finish off the seat by applying a medium-grade sandpaper to the surfaces as the seat continues turning at high speed, never holding the paper in one position for too long, but moving it continuously until the top of the seat and its round edge are perfectly smooth. Owing to the heat that is generated between the spinning wood and the abrasive paper,

you will probably need to wear a glove to protect your fingers, and a respirator should be placed over the nose and mouth so that you do not inhale any of the copious dust that fills the atmosphere. The final stage of sandpapering should be with a fine-grade sheet.

When you are satisfied with the appearance of the stool seat, remove it from the face-plate of the lathe, together with the second wooden block, and separate the two by gently prising into the cardboard interface with the tip of a broad chisel. As the card tears apart, some of it will be left adhering to the underside of the seat, and this can be removed by thoroughly rubbing down with medium-grade sandpaper until all traces of card and wood glue have been eradicated.

The next step is to make the four stool legs and four rails, all of which conform to a pattern. There are various ways of decorating a long cylindrical chair or stool leg to relieve the monotony of a plain round surface, and you might well have ideas of your own in this respect. The style adopted in this example, and indeed in the kitchen chair which appears elsewhere in the book, is to arrange for a series of 'bobbins' along the length of each leg, and a single 'bobbin' at the centre of each rail, in which each 'bobbin' merely consists of two lines cut into the wood, separated by a gap of 25mm (1in), and the edges cut to a V-shape with the parting tool and rounded off with a narrow gouge. The diameter of each 'bobbin' remains the same as that of the neighbouring wood, except for the ends of the legs, which taper slightly.

Commencing with the four legs, each of these is turned from a length of mopstick material, which is normally in-

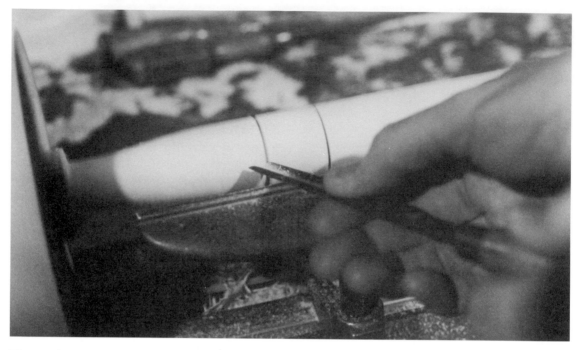

The stool leg is turned in the lathe and the decorative 'bobbin' effect applied with a narrow gouge.

tended for use as a handrail, already being turned into a near-perfect circle with a single flattened edge. Mopstick is prepared from softwood, measures about 45mm (1¾in) in diameter, and is stocked by most timber merchants and some DIY stores. Its chief advantage as far as we are concerned is that the first stage of wood-turning, which usually entails roughing out a square-section length of timber into a rounded shape, is not necessary in this instance: instead, you simply need to cut the mopstick to the required length, with flat ends, measure the centre of each end-grain and mount the mopstick in the lathe.

Alternatively, if softwood material is already available, each leg can be turned from wood measuring 45 × 45mm (1¾ × 1¾in) in cross-section. Mark the centre of

each end-grain by drawing two straight lines between diagonally opposite corners, and mount securely in the lathe. Now, the initial stage of wood-turning consists of removing the four corners of the wood with the parting tool and the spindle gouge so that it is roughed out in the form of a cylinder.

Whichever way you begin, whether it is with mopstick or square-section material, each piece must be cut somewhat longer than the length of the finished leg, so that there is ample material for the joint to be formed at the top, and for the 'casting off' at each end. As the length of the finished leg measures 660mm (26in), plus an extra 16mm (⅝in) at the top for the jointing peg that fits into a hole drilled in the underside of the seat, an overall length of 710mm (28in) is desirable.

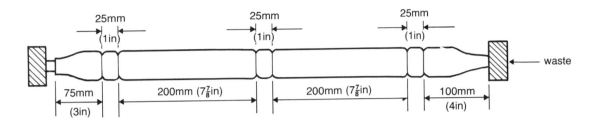

Dimensions of the stool legs.

Turn the wood to a diameter slightly more than the 35mm (1⅜in) diameter of the finished leg, checking with a simple measuring gauge cut from stiff card which has a gap of 38mm (1½in) set in it. Measure and mark off the full length of the leg, including the additional 16mm (⅝in) at the top for the peg, and mark in the positions of the three 'bobbins' that decorate the leg, placing these where you think they look most effective.

Shape the 'bobbins' with the parting tool and the narrow gouge, as already described, and taper off both ends of the leg, finally reducing the topmost portion for the peg to a diameter of 19mm (¾in).

Switch off the lathe and examine the surface of the leg: you will see that it is quite rough with grain raised in places, and wood fibres gouged out in others, rather similar to the texture of sawn wood. Certainly this can be refined further by more wood-turning, but you must be careful not to reduce the diameter of the leg much more, otherwise it will end up being narrower than you want – and even then it will still need to be sandpapered.

The alternative technique is to lay down the wood-turning tools when the diameter of the leg is approximately 38mm (1½in) and remove the remaining 3mm (⅛in) with abrasive paper. This does not mean ordinary sandpaper, which quickly loses its roughened surface, but a heavier, more expensive material used in floor-sanding machines and similar appliances. You should be able to obtain a couple of sheets from a tool-hire shop. Divide these up into smaller pieces with a sharp knife, starting with a medium-grit paper to cut quickly into the surface of the leg, then changing to a fine-grit.

Keep stopping the lathe to check the diameter of the leg using another card gauge set to a gap of 35mm (1⅜in).

Retrim the 'bobbins' with the parting tool and the narrow gouge, and complete the rubbing down with fine-grade ordinary sandpaper, still with the lathe running. Once you are satisfied with the first leg, remove it from the lathe and proceed with the remaining three; but do not trim off the waste from the ends until all four legs have been prepared because you might find it necessary to remount them in the lathe and trim a little more here and there so that they are all identical. The waste should finally be removed with the tenon saw, remembering to leave 16mm (⅝in) for the pin at the top of each leg.

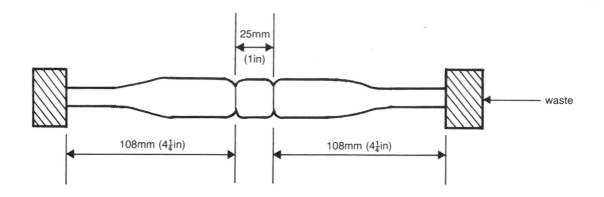

25mm
(1in)

waste

108mm (4¼in)   108mm (4¼in)

Dimensions of the rails.

The four leg rails are prepared in the same way, except that as these are smaller in diameter you do not need to make them from mopstick, but may instead turn them from softwood measuring 32 × 32mm (1¼ × 1¼in). The four identical legs, when eventually fitted to the seat, are mounted so that

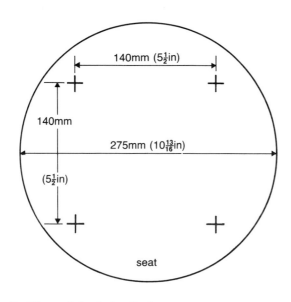

140mm (5½in)

140mm

275mm (10¹³⁄₁₆in)

(5½in)

seat

Positions of the holes in the seat.

they splay outwards for stability, and the four rails should each be turned to a length of 242mm (9½in), with a maximum diameter at the centre of 22mm (⅞in) tapering to a diameter at each end of 16mm (⅝in), with a 'bobbin' measuring 25mm (1in) long at the centre.

All of the stool components are now ready for assembly. The four 19mm (¾in) diameter holes that are to be drilled in the underside of the seat, to receive the pins at the ends of the legs, are marked so that their centres occur at the four corners of an imaginary square, a distance of 140mm (5½in) being equal to each side of the square. With their positions marked, lay the seat upside down on the workbench and drill out each hole with a 19mm (¾in) diameter centre bit mounted in the handbrace, angling the drill in such a manner that it splays outwards in the same direction as that intended for the leg. Bore to a depth of 19mm (¾in), checking as you drill to ensure that the tip of the bit does not begin to break through on the upper surface of the seat.

Next, measure and mark the two adjacent hole positions in each leg, setting all

The four holes for the legs are drilled in the underside of the seat with the 19mm ($\frac{3}{4}$in) diameter centre bit, each one angled slightly outwards.

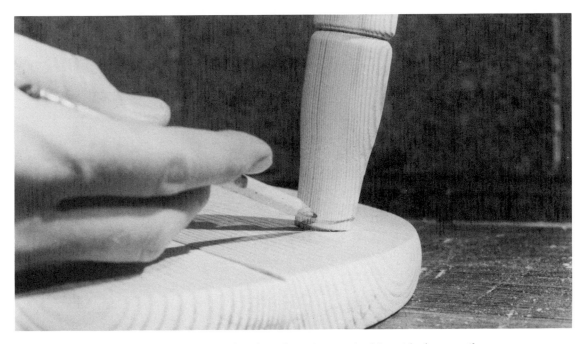

The leg is loosely fitted into its hole and a sloped portion marked in with the pencil before trimming.

Assembling the leg rails to the legs of the stool.

can imagine it that way, to make allowance for the legs diverging outwards while the rails are mounted horizontally, boring with a 16mm ($\frac{5}{8}$in) diameter centre bit to a depth of 13mm ($\frac{1}{2}$in), whereupon you will discover that the two holes meet within the wood.

Before the legs and the rails can be properly attached to one another, and fitted to the seat, it is desirable to trim in two respects: firstly, at the top of each leg, and the shoulder beneath the pin may be sloped fractionally so that it butts perfectly up against the underside of the seat when the leg is assembled into its hole; and, secondly, the ends of the rails can be mitred, or bevelled, so that they sit fully within their receiver holes.

Mix a quantity of wood glue, apply it by brush to all of the holes, to the pins of the legs and the ends of each rail, and assemble the stool, tapping all of the joints fully home and checking that the seat is level before leaving the glue to set hard.

After the glue has dried and hardened completely, rub down all the surfaces of the stool with fine-grade sandpaper and apply your chosen finish.

of these 230mm (9in) up from the bottom end of the leg. Drill at a slight upward angle towards the top of the leg, if you

CHAPTER FOUR

BATHROOM CABINET

The design of this cabinet follows a standard pattern, being of a rectangular shape and fitted with two hinged doors, each containing a single mirror panel. The interior has one shelf, mounted in a position which allows for the storage of tall bottles along the bottom with smaller items above.

Begin by marking out the four lengths required for the top, bottom and two side panels. In measuring the sides, be sure to allow an extra 9mm ($\frac{3}{8}$in) at each end for the tenon. Square off with a pencil, and cut each piece to size with the tenon saw.

The next step is to refine them further with an attractive edge-moulding, using the electric router or plough plane fitted with a suitable cutter. Probably the best profile for the cabinet is the corner-round pattern. Fit the appropriate cutter into the tool, adjusting the depth of the cut and the position of the guide-fence to give the desired effect. It is a good idea to experiment using a length of scrap wood identical in thickness to that of the top, bottom and side panels.

When you are satisfied with the result of the trial edge-moulding, prepare to work the same profile along the two end-grains and the front edge of both the top and bottom panels. Taking each piece in turn, clamp the material securely to the end of the workbench, and make the first

Cutting list

The Cabinet

Top panel: one of 610 × 145 × 19mm (24 × 5$\frac{3}{4}$ × $\frac{3}{4}$in)
Bottom panel: one of 610 × 145 × 19mm (24 × 5$\frac{3}{4}$ × $\frac{3}{4}$in)
Side panels: two of 383 × 137 × 19mm (15$\frac{1}{8}$ × 5$\frac{3}{8}$ × $\frac{3}{4}$in)
Shelf: one of 545 × 100 × 19mm (21$\frac{1}{2}$ × 4 × $\frac{3}{4}$in)
Back panel: one of 560 × 380 × 4mm (22 × 15 × $\frac{3}{16}$in)
Door stile: four of 360 × 34 × 19mm (14$\frac{3}{16}$ × 1$\frac{3}{8}$ × $\frac{3}{4}$in) rebated
Door rail: four of 253 × 34 × 19mm (10 × 1$\frac{3}{8}$ × $\frac{3}{4}$in) rebated
Door panel: two of 300 × 215 × 2mm (11$\frac{13}{16}$ × 8$\frac{1}{16}$ × $\frac{3}{32}$in)

The Towel Rail

Backplate: one of 610 × 70 × 19mm (24 × 2$\frac{3}{4}$ × $\frac{3}{4}$in)
Arm: two of 100 × 60 × 19mm (4 × 2$\frac{3}{8}$ × $\frac{3}{4}$in)
Rail: one of 590 × 16mm (23$\frac{1}{4}$ × $\frac{5}{8}$in) diameter

The Toilet Roll Holder

Backplate: one of 222 × 70 × 19mm (8$\frac{3}{4}$ × 2$\frac{3}{4}$ × $\frac{3}{4}$in)
Arm: two of 100 × 60 × 19mm (4 × 2$\frac{3}{8}$ × $\frac{3}{4}$in)
Rail: one of 210 × 16mm (8$\frac{1}{4}$ × $\frac{5}{8}$in) diameter

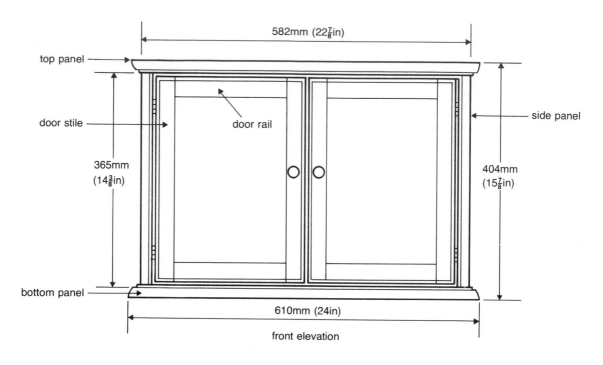

582mm (22⅞in)

top panel

door stile

door rail

side panel

365mm
(14⅜in)

404mm
(15⅞in)

bottom panel

610mm (24in)

front elevation

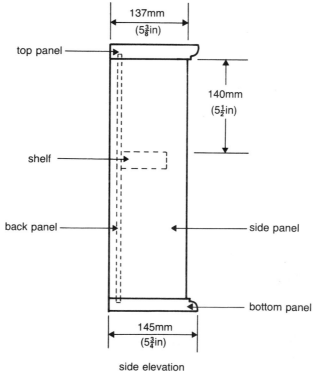

137mm
(5⅜in)

top panel

140mm
(5½in)

shelf

back panel

side panel

bottom panel

145mm
(5¾in)

side elevation

Main dimensions of the bathroom cabinet.

cuts across the end-grain. It is best not to try to achieve the desired profile by making a single cut with the router set at the maximum depth, but to work the tool several times, firstly with a very shallow cut, increasing the depth each time so that only small amounts of wood are removed, thus avoiding a tendency for the cutter to become overheated and scorch the soft grain.

The end-grains are prepared first because there is always the possibility that some of the wood will splinter away at the far edge as the cutter completes its run. This may be avoided by clamping a piece of scrap wood tightly up against the panel being cut, forming a continuation of the end-grain, so that if any splintering is to occur, it will happen to the scrap piece, which must obviously be of the same thickness and have its end cut square.

Once the two end-grains have been prepared satisfactorily, turn the panel lengthways and make the final cut along the grain of the front edge. If the tool has been manipulated accurately, the corner-round profiles should match perfectly at both front corners.

The two side panels are given an identical moulding pattern along the corner between the front edge and the outside face. Note that although the sides were originally cut from the same 145 × 19mm (5¾ × ¾in) material, the required width is actually only 137mm (5⅜in) to allow for

The router makes its final edge-moulding cut along the grain of the front edge of the top and bottom panel.

the fact that the front edge of the two sides is set back by 8mm (⅜in) from the front edge of the top and bottom panels, the rear edges all being flush.

Set the marking gauge to a gap of 8mm (⅜in) and scribe a line along both faces of the side panels, working the fence of the gauge along the rear edges of the material, and plane off the waste until both sides are reduced to the required width.

The two sides are fitted to the top and bottom panels with mortise and tenon joints, the mortises being cut on the underside of the top panel and the upper surface of the bottom panel. A matching tenon is cut at each end of the two sides.

Mark in the mortises first. As you will observe, the top and bottom panels are arranged so that the edge-mouldings are directed inwards towards the centre of the cabinet. The object is to ensure that the outer face of the side panels is set in by 5mm (³⁄₁₆in) from the lip of the moulding. Once the line determining the outward position of the side panels has been marked in, it is easy to measure the mortise position, pencilling in two parallel lines with the square, with a 6mm (¼in) gap in between. Finally, set in the ends of the mortise by 6mm (¼in).

The cutting out of the four mortises can be performed quickly with the router, fitted with a 6mm (¼in) diameter straight cutter. The method is much the same as that of cutting out a housing groove – indeed, this joint has much in

Use the router to remove the bulk of the waste from each mortise in the top and bottom panel, guiding it along a straight-edged piece of wood.

Cut the rounded ends of the mortise perfectly square with the 6mm (¼in) chisel.

common with the housing joint – except that in this instance the groove is stopped at each end to create the mortise. Set the fence of the router to place its cutter accurately within the marked parallel lines of the mortise, and adjust the depth gauge to produce a cut 9mm (⅜in) deep. Work the router carefully between the two ends of the mortise, and where the cutter starts and finishes its run, leaving a rounded end, chop each end square with the 6mm (¼in) chisel.

If you prefer not to use the router for this purpose, the mortise may be prepared firstly by drilling a series of 6mm (¼in) diameter holes with an auger bit mounted in a handbrace, boring to a depth of 9mm (⅜in), and then carefully chopping out the waste with the 6mm (¼in) chisel and a mallet. Make sure that the chisel blade has a very sharp cutting edge; otherwise, in cutting across the grain, you could easily produce a rough, ragged edge in close proximity to the carefully-prepared edge-moulding.

Now mark the tenons at the ends of the two side panels. Begin by setting the mortise gauge to a gap of 6mm (¼in) between the two spurs, and adjust the fence to centralize the pointers across the thickness of the end-grain. Scribe two parallel lines along the ends, setting the shoulder lines to a distance of 9mm (⅜in) from either end. Remove the waste with the tenon saw in the usual way, and cut in the third and fourth shoulders to a depth of 6mm (¼in) so that the tenons match exactly the size of the mortises.

Tap the four joints experimentally together to form the carcase of the cabinet, checking that each joint fits fully home, and trimming where necessary with the chisel if any of the joints do not quite mate as they should.

Now measure in the housing groove for the back panel along the rear inside face of each of the top, bottom and side panels. The back panel is cut from a sheet of white-faced hardboard and measures 4mm ($\frac{3}{16}$in) thick, but it is advisable to cut the groove to a width of 6mm ($\frac{1}{4}$in) and a depth of 9mm ($\frac{3}{8}$in), using the same cutter as that employed for the mortises. Cut the housing grooves between the mortises at each end of the top and bottom panels, and along the full length of the side panels.

Mark out the rectangular back panel on the sheet of white-faced hardboard, allowing for the extra height and width needed to fit into the housing grooves. Score along the marked lines with a sharp knife so that when you cut out the panel using a jig-saw or handsaw, the blade of the saw will not lift and tear off any of the brittle white coating.

Cut a piece of household greaseproof paper to the same size as the back panel, and gum it to the extreme edges of the panel using a paper adhesive, so that the greaseproof sheet completely covers the white facing of the hardboard. This is to protect the back panel once it has been assembled to the rest of the cabinet from being accidentally covered in varnish during the finishing stages.

Slot the back panel, with its protective covering, into its grooves and once again temporarily assemble the four main components of the cabinet. Provided it has been cut with its four corners square, the presence of the back panel now ensures that all the corners of the cabinet form perfect right-angles.

Stick the piece of greaseproof paper to the extreme edges of the back panel.

Make a trial assembly of the main components of the cabinet to check that
the joints fit properly together, and to measure accurately the required length of
the interior shelf.

Measure the distance between the inside faces of the side panels, which gives the exact required length of the interior shelf. The width of this shelf is 100mm (4in) to take account of the back panel and the thickness of the cabinet doors. Cut the shelf to size, planing down the edges. Its position within the cabinet is largely a matter of personal choice, and you should decide for yourself what proportion of space you want to have above and below it. But as a guide, you will probably find it most convenient to locate the shelf two-fifths of the way down from the top of the interior of the cabinet.

The shelf is fixed to the sides with dowel joints, two 6mm (¼in) diameter dowels being fitted at each end. Set the marking gauge so that the distance between its fence and its spur is equal to exactly half the thickness of the shelf, and scribe a line across each end-grain. Mark in the positions of the dowels along this line, setting their centres in by a distance of 19mm (¾in) from the front and rear edges of the shelf. Mark the corresponding hole positions on the inside face of each side panel, checking that they are set equally down from the top. Drill the holes to a depth of 13mm (½in) in the side panels, and 19mm (¾in) into the end-grain of the shelf, using a 6mm (¼in) diameter auger bit in the handbrace.

Cut four pieces of 6mm (¼in) diameter dowel to a length of just under 32mm (1¼in) each, chamfering the ends slightly in a pencil sharpener, and lightly sawing

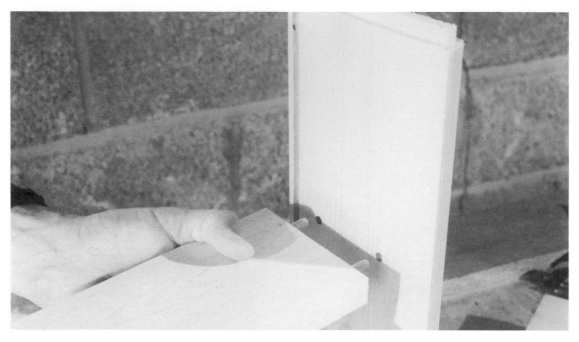

Assembling the interior shelf to the side panel with a dowel joint.

The two side panels and the interior shelf form an H-pattern, and this sub-assembly is fitted to the bottom panel.

The back panel is slotted into its grooves.

along their length to make a shallow glue channel.

Dismantle the cabinet again and thoroughly sandpaper all the surfaces of the wood, switching from medium to fine-grade paper. Mix some wood glue, and begin by joining the shelf to the two side panels, forming an H-shape. Next, glue the mortise and tenon joints between the sides and the bottom panel, and tap these fully home. Insert the back panel carefully into its grooves and push it down as far as it will go, making sure that the edges of the greaseproof paper do not detach or crease. Finally, glue the top panel joints and fit them tightly together. Wipe away any traces of glue which may have squeezed out from the joints, cramp up the assembly and stand

it to one side for the requisite period of time while the glue hardens completely.

The two cabinet doors are made from lengths of rebated 34 × 19mm (1$\frac{3}{8}$ × $\frac{3}{4}$in) material, each rebate being cut 6mm ($\frac{1}{4}$in) into the width of the wood, and 13mm ($\frac{1}{2}$in) across the thickness.

Taking each door individually, mark out the two stiles, adding a little extra at either end as a safety margin. Measure the two rails, allowing for the tenons, and cut these to length. Set the pointers of the mortise gauge to a gap of 6mm ($\frac{1}{4}$in) and adjust the fence until the pointers are placed to mark two parallel lines midway across the thickness of the material, as it was previously set to mark the tenons at the ends of the two side panels.

Mark in the mortises at the ends of the

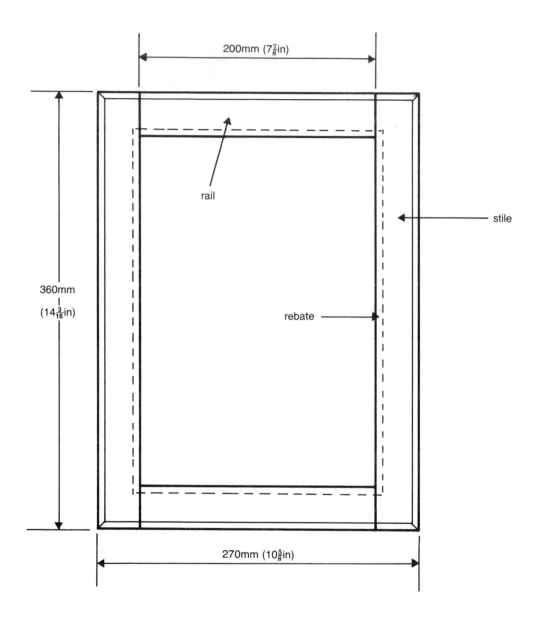

Main dimensions of the cabinet doors.

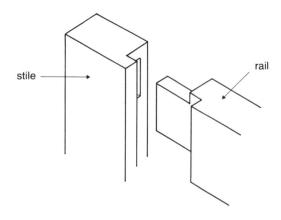

Use mortise and tenon joints for the door frame.

stiles, and the matching tenons at the ends of the rails, noting that the rebate causes the tenons to have offset shoulders. Set in the mortises by 9mm (⅜in) at each end and cut them to a depth of 19mm (¾in) from the surface of the rebate. Prepare them in the customary manner of firstly drilling out most of the waste with the 6mm (¼in) auger bit, chopping out the remainder with the 6mm (¼in) chisel and the mallet, and removing the waste from the tenons with the tenon saw.

Before gluing the door frame together, mark and cut out a rectangle from thick card of such a size that it fits precisely into the rebates, so that, knowing the corners of the card to be perfectly square, the corners of the door frame can be guaranteed to form right-angles. Mix a small quantity of wood glue, brush it into the mortise and tenon joints, and assemble the door frame – its card template fitted in position – and cramp up the assembly. Once the glue has dried and set hard, tap out the template, removing any traces of card which might have

adhered to the inside of the rebate using the blade of the chisel.

Saw off the projecting excess material from the ends of the stiles, bringing them squarely into line with the rails by planing lightly. Using the same edge-moulding cutter as for the main components of the cabinet, work a matching profile along the four outside corners of the door between the front face and the four outer edges. Remember the rule about cutting across the grain first so that the top and bottom rails, together with the end-grains of the stiles, are cut to begin with. Due to the relative fragility of the door frame, it is important to clamp lengths of waste wood at each side, the waste material being equal in thickness to the rails and stiles, so that, as previously, the router cutter does not cause the edges of the end-grain to splinter as the router finishes its run.

Cut a corner-round edge-moulding on the four outside corners of each door frame.

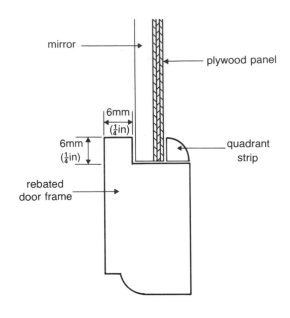

mirror

plywood panel

6mm
($\frac{1}{4}$in)

6mm
($\frac{1}{4}$in)

quadrant
strip

rebated
door frame

Method of attaching the mirror to the
door frame.

Measure the size of the two mirrors so that they fit comfortably into the rebates, and order the 4mm ($\frac{3}{16}$in) thick mirror from your local glass supplier. Also purchase four 38mm (1$\frac{1}{2}$in) brass butt hinges.

Cut two shallow recesses in the outer stile of each door to receive the hinges, with corresponding recesses on the inside face of the side panels, into which the flaps of the hinges are securely screwed.

Apply several coats of satin varnish throughout the cabinet, allowing each coat to dry completely before rubbing down with very fine sandpaper or wire wool and brushing on the next coat. When the final coat has hardened to the desired finish, remove the greaseproof paper from the back panel by tearing it and pulling it out.

Fit the mirrors into their rebates and

cover them entirely at the back with matching-sized panels of thin pine-coloured plywood to protect the silvering from getting scratched. Glue lengths of small quadrant moulding between the plywood and the edges of the rebates to hold the mirror and the plywood backing in place, mitring the ends of the quadrant for a neat finish.

Fit small pine door knobs, and either magnetic or ball catches to keep the doors closed.

Finally, drill two 4mm ($\frac{3}{16}$in) diameter holes in the white-faced hardboard panel to take the fixing screws used to attach the cabinet to the bathroom wall, and glue rubber washers behind the holes to take up the gap between the back of the panel and the wall.

BATHROOM ACCESSORIES

By now, you will probably have accumulated quite a lot of off-cut material from the items you have already made. A special bin to keep all the short lengths of usable wood can often prove a wonderful source of supply for smaller items, such as a pine towel rail and toilet-roll holder which match perfectly with the bathroom cabinet to create an attractive ensemble.

Both items are smaller in design and identical in the method of construction, each having a backplate, two arms, a cylindrical rail or spindle, and two knobs. In the case of the towel rail, the two knobs should be fixed permanently to the ends of the rail, but with the toilet-roll holder one knob must remain detachable so that the spindle can easily be withdrawn in order to change rolls.

Start by making the backplate, cutting it to the required length from a piece of

70 × 19mm (2¾ × ¾in) material. All four front corners have a corner-round edge-moulding worked along them, using the electric router fitted with the appropriate cutter. Begin by working the profile on the two end-grains, clamping the piece securely to the end of the workbench. As it is rather difficult to cut across the grain without causing the wood to splinter off towards the end of the router's passage, it is a good idea to take a second piece of wood – of identical thickness to the backplate and sufficiently long to permit its square-cut end-grain to be clamped flush with the end-grain of the backplate – so that as the router works its way across the wood, it continues on to the scrap material and thus does not split the backplate.

Having completed the ends satisfactorily, you will find that the backplate is not wide enough to allow you to run the router along the two lengthways edges, as the clamps that fasten the material to the end of the workbench would interfere with the movement of the router and prevent it from making a single clean cut. The best way to get around this problem is to mark in and drill the two No. 8 mounting-holes used to attach the backplate to the bathroom wall, and screw the piece firmly to a block of scrap wood which is substantial enough to be gripped by the vice, providing the necessary clearance for the router to make an uninterrupted run along the grain.

Use a similar method to prepare the same moulding pattern on the front end-

The backplate for the towel rail is screwed to a block of scrap wood which is, in turn, clamped firmly to the workbench, thus allowing the router to pass fully along the length of the piece.

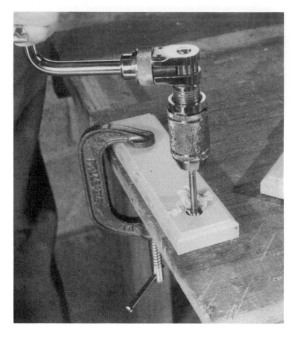

Drill a hole in each arm to receive the towel rail or toilet roll spindle. At this stage, the arms are still cut overlength.

Assembling the two arms to the backplate.

grain and the two edges of each arm. The rear end is cut square with the tenon saw so that it can be butted up at right-angles to the backplate. Note that each arm is 9mm (⅜in) narrower overall than the backplate so that the upper and lower edges lie flush with the lip of the corner round profile.

Mark in the position of the hole for the rail or spindle in both arms and drill out the waste using a 16mm (⅝in) diameter centre bit. Bore firstly from the outer surface until the point of the bit just breaks through on the opposite side and, turning the piece over, complete the drilling. Pass a length of 16mm (⅝in) diameter dowelling through the hole to check that there is adequate room for it to fit and turn without binding. In the event of the dowelling sticking within the hole, enlarge its diameter slightly with a round file.

Place the two arms in their positions at each end of the backplate, setting them at least 3mm (⅛in) inside the two screw holes. Mark in two dowel joints used to fix each arm to the backplate. The dowel holes should be drilled to a diameter of 6mm (¼in) and a depth of 13mm (½in), with the dowels each cut to a length of 25mm (1in) and the ends chamfered in a pencil sharpener.

Rub down all three components with fine sandpaper, then mix a small amount of wood glue and apply it to the joints with a small brush, assembling the dowels into their holes, and ensuring that the two arms fit tightly up against the backplate and lie perpendicular to it.

Purchase a pair of pine door knobs to match the style of those fitted to the doors of the bathroom cabinet, checking that the diameter of the stem is wide enough to allow for a 16mm (⅝in) dia-

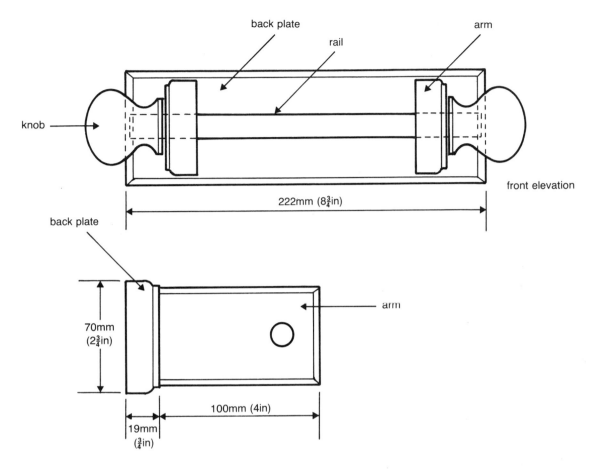

Main dimensions of the toilet roll holder.

meter hole to be drilled in the centre of the flat end to a depth of 19mm (¾in). The knobs will need to be held very firmly in the workbench vice, or some similar clamping contrivance, to stop them from turning with the motion of the hand-brace, and this may tend to flatten them slightly on their rounded surfaces. A rub down with medium-grade sandpaper ought to restore the original contour.

Cut the 16mm (⅝in) diameter towel rail to length, measuring for the additional 19mm (¾in) required at each end to fit into the knob. Both towel rail knobs need to be attached with either glue, or a small fastening peg driven into a tiny hole drilled through the knob and the rail combined. Of course, in the case of the toilet roll holder only one knob should be secured, the second knob remaining easily detachable for the frequent replacing of used rolls.

Apply the same wood finish as that given to the cabinet, except for the rail or spindle, which is given a thorough rub down with good-quality wax polish to produce a shiny surface and to reduce friction inside the two mounting holes.

CHAPTER FIVE

BEDSIDE CABINET

If you want to give your bedroom a country look, you cannot do better than to furnish it with pine cabinets. Simple in design, each cabinet is made from jointed boards for its main panels, and has three useful drawers of traditional construction. Decoration is provided by the ornamented ledge at the rear of the top shelf, and the curved feet.

Start by making the boards from which you will cut the top, bottom and side panels. There are two ways in which the boards may be prepared: you can either purchase tongued-and-grooved planks, and slot several lengths together without having to prepare any joints, or you can use plain boards and cut your own joints to make them fit to the required overall width.

In the former instance, tongued-and-grooved material measuring 140×19mm ($5\frac{1}{2} \times \frac{3}{4}$in) should be used, in which case three separate pieces will be needed to make up the total width; but if you choose the latter course and make up your own joints, use four lengths of 122×19mm ($4\frac{3}{4} \times \frac{3}{4}$in) material, joined edge to edge. In either case, measure and cut the boards to a length of 530mm ($20\frac{7}{8}$in), and arrange them side by side so that the annular rings which are plainly visible on the end-grain alternate in the direction of rotation from one board to the next. The

Cutting List

Top shelf: one of $510 \times 410 \times 19$mm ($20\frac{1}{8} \times 16\frac{1}{8} \times \frac{3}{4}$in)

Bottom panel: one of $510 \times 410 \times 19$mm ($20\frac{1}{8} \times 16\frac{1}{8} \times \frac{3}{4}$in)

Side: two of $510 \times 390 \times 19$mm ($20\frac{1}{8} \times 15\frac{3}{8} \times \frac{3}{4}$in)

Ledge: one of $460 \times 75 \times 19$mm ($18\frac{1}{8} \times 3 \times \frac{3}{4}$in)

Foot: eight of $125 \times 45 \times 19$mm ($4\frac{7}{8} \times 1\frac{3}{4} \times \frac{3}{4}$in)

Back panel: one of $522 \times 458 \times 6$mm ($20\frac{1}{2} \times 18 \times \frac{1}{4}$in)

Drawer rail: four of $442 \times 45 \times 19$mm ($17\frac{3}{8} \times 1\frac{3}{4} \times \frac{3}{4}$in)

Drawer runner: eight of $332 \times 19 \times 19$mm ($13\frac{1}{8} \times \frac{3}{4} \times \frac{3}{4}$in)

Drawer front: three of $434 \times 145 \times 19$mm ($17\frac{1}{8} \times 5\frac{3}{4} \times \frac{3}{4}$in)

Drawer back: three of $434 \times 145 \times 19$mm ($17\frac{1}{8} \times 5\frac{3}{4} \times \frac{3}{4}$in)

Drawer side: six of $370 \times 145 \times 19$mm ($14\frac{9}{16} \times 5\frac{3}{4} \times \frac{3}{4}$in)

Drawer bottom: three of $404 \times 344 \times 6$mm ($15\frac{7}{8} \times 9\frac{9}{16} \times \frac{1}{4}$in)

purpose of this is to counteract to some degree the tendency of any single piece to bend slightly as it dries.

Ready-prepared tongued-and-grooved boards simply require a small amount of wood glue to be brushed into their grooves and on the surfaces of their

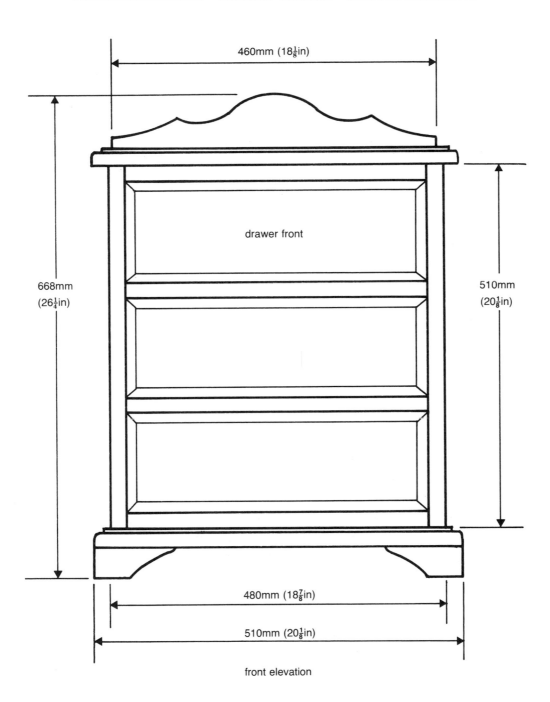

460mm (18⅛in)

668mm (26¼in)

drawer front

510mm (20⅛in)

480mm (18⅞in)

510mm (20⅛in)

front elevation

Main dimensions of the bedside cabinet.

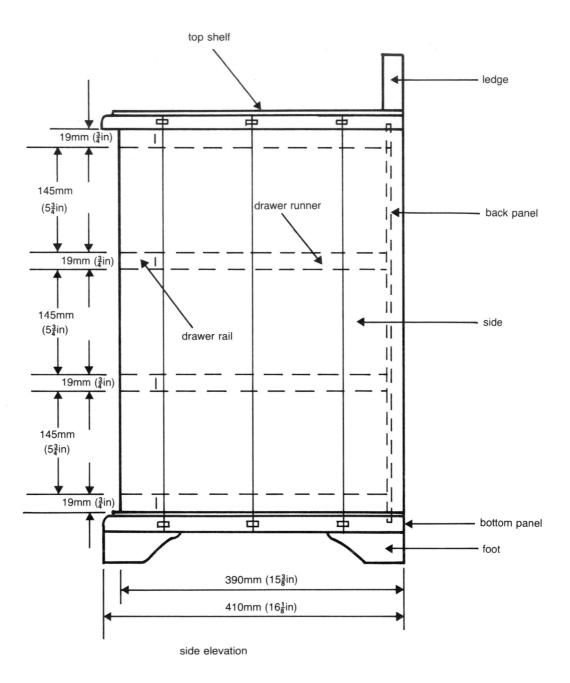

side elevation

The bedside cabinet – side view.

Cut a groove along the joining edges of the boards, using the router fitted with a 6mm ($\frac{1}{4}$in) diameter cutter.

Apply wood glue thoroughly to the grooves cut in the boards.

tongues, and the boards fitted tightly together and – while ensuring that they are perfectly flat – cramped together for the period of time necessary for the glue to set hard.

The alternative method of joining the plain boards together is by using what might be called the loose tongue joint. The tongue is a strip of hardwood measuring 13 × 6mm ($\frac{1}{2} \times \frac{1}{4}$in), which you can purchase in long lengths from timber stockists, and the receiving groove is cut in the edge of the boards with a router or plough plane fitted with a 6mm ($\frac{1}{4}$in) cutter. Each groove should be 6mm ($\frac{1}{4}$in) deep – or perhaps very slightly more – to accommodate the tongue.

Mark in the positions of the grooves on each board's adjoining edge by setting the two pointers of the mortise gauge to a gap of 6mm ($\frac{1}{4}$in), and adjusting the fence until the marks made by the gauge are set centrally on the edge. Scribe a pair of parallel lines along each edge.

Clamp the material firmly in the workbench vice and prepare the grooves with the router or plough plane, ensuring that the cutter works within the gauged lines.

Cut the 13 × 6mm ($\frac{1}{2} \times \frac{1}{4}$in) hardwood into pieces each measuring 530mm (20$\frac{7}{8}$in) long. Mix some wood glue and apply it to the grooves with a small brush, tapping the tongues into place and pressing the joints fully home. As each composite board has four individual lengths of plank to it, there will be a total of three joins. Cramp up the board to hold the joints tightly together while the

Fit the loose tongue into its grooves, and assemble the separate boards into a single panel.

glue dries and hardens, wiping away any surplus glue that has squeezed out from the joins with a damp cloth.

After a day, remove the cramps and thoroughly sandpaper the two surfaces of each board to remove traces of glue and to smooth out the joins where necessary. Inevitably there will be tiny lines to show where the joins occur, but these are an acceptable part of the design and no attempt should be made to fill the gaps which should, in any case, only be marginal.

Having made the four boards, select the best of them from which to make the top shelf. This implies a certain degree of personal choice, because you might want a liberal sprinkling of knots, or perhaps you prefer a board with larger but fewer knots which are relatively pale in colour

and not too obtrusive. Measure the chosen board to the required 510mm (20⅛in) length, marking in the lines with a square straight-edge and pencil. By firstly making the board overlong, and then cutting it to its correct length, you should produce clean square end-grains. Remove the waste with the handsaw or electric jig-saw – the jig-saw being the preferred tool as it produces a very fine cut. Finish off by planing the end-grain.

Follow the same procedure to reduce the width of the board to the required amount, removing equal waste from the front and rear edges so that the faintly visible joint lines are symmetrical.

The board is now ready to have an edging pattern worked along both end-grains and the front edge. The edging is best cut with the router, and you have a choice of profile according to which type of cutter you fit. The corner-round cutter is probably the most suitable, if not necessarily the most ornate.

Set up the router so that the cutter works to a predetermined depth, with the fence adjusted so that the commencing of the cut just coincides in line with the edge of the board, then clamp the top shelf to the end of the workbench and run the router across the two end-grains of the board before finishing with the front edge. There is a purpose in adopting this order: when you make a cut of any sort across the exposed end-grain, the cutting blade, as it approaches the far end of the material, often splinters off a small portion. This can, admittedly, be counteracted by clamping a piece of scrap material tightly up against the far edge – the material having precisely the same thickness, and a straight-cut end-grain – so that as the router progresses along its path, it continues uninterrupted on to the scrap wood, leaving the top shelf with a perfect cut.

Rather than try to cut the edge-moulding in a single run of the router, which could cause the cutter to overheat and scorch the wood, make several runs, starting with only very gentle downward pressure on the tool, gradually increasing until you attain the full depth. Although more time-consuming, the chances are that the final profile will be more even and free from scorch marks.

When all three edges have been cut satisfactorily, rub down gently with sandpaper to remove all the small stands of wood left behind by the spinning cutter. Always rub in the direction of the grain, otherwise the surface will appear scratched.

Next, select a board for the bottom panel which, because most of it will be out of sight in the finished cabinet, does not have to be of the highest quality, and prepare it carefully to the same shape and size as the top shelf.

The two sides are also 510mm (20⅛in) long and should be sawn and planed to length, but their width is slightly less

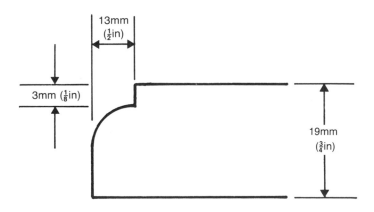

Dimensions of the corner round moulding.

than that of the top shelf and bottom panel. However, great care should be taken to match up the joint lines, as the finished cabinet will look of higher quality if the lines – faint as they may well be – follow a regular pattern throughout. More waste will therefore need to be removed from the front edge of the side panels than from the rear.

The grooves that receive the plywood backing panel should now be prepared. The method is the same as for cutting the grooves in the edges of the individual boards to receive the loose tongue, since the plywood is of the same 6mm (¼in) thickness. Fit the 6mm (¼in) diameter straight cutter back in the router and adjust the fence to give a distance of 9mm (⅜in) between the housing groove and the rear edge of the panel. Cut to a depth of 6mm (¼in).

Taking each side panel in turn, work the groove along the full length of the inside surface adjacent to the rear edge. When this is completed, place the two sides in position on the top shelf and bottom panel respectively, set in by 6mm (¼in) from the innermost shoulder of the corner-round edge-moulding, and mark in the depths of the grooves in pencil. These marks give you the limits to which the grooves must be cut on the underside of the top shelf, and the upper surface of the bottom panel. Take care not to mix these up by mistake.

Cut the backing panel from a sheet of 6mm (¼in) thick plywood, selecting a type of ply that matches well with the pale colour of pine, and make sure that you allow for the extra amounts needed to fill the housing grooves. Make a trial assembly of the five components thus far completed to check that all is well up to this point.

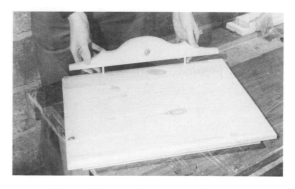

Assemble the ledge to the rear of the top shelf with dowels and wood glue.

Prepare a template for the ledge from a piece of stiff card, the curves being drawn symmetrically about a centre-line using an artist's French curves, or some such similar drawing aid, cutting the template to shape with a sharp knife and transferring the outline on to a length of material. Cut out the pattern on the wood using the jig-saw or coping saw, finishing if need be with the spokeshave before sandpapering the curved edging smooth. The ledge is then fitted to the rear surface of the top shelf with the dowel joints. These are cut from 6mm (¼in) diameter dowelling, and their receiver holes drilled with a 6mm (¼in) diameter auger bit to a depth of 13mm (½in) in the top shelf and 19mm (¾in) in the ledge, setting in the dowel-hole positions approximately 100mm (4in) from the ends of the ledge. Take care to prevent the drilling of the holes in the top shelf from interfering with the housing groove for the back panel. If either of the holes should break through into the groove, ensure during the assembling of the ledge to the top shelf that the dowel does not protrude into the groove but remains flush with it.

Cut the four drawer rails to length

from 45 × 19mm (1¾ × ¾in) material, and the eight drawer runners from 19 × 19mm (¾ × ¾in) material. There are four separate levels at which these rails and runners are fitted, splitting the cabinet up into three equal parts. Indeed, the topmost rail and runners serve no other purpose than to balance their counterparts at the bottom of the cabinet, since they play no part in supporting the top drawer, although their presence, of course, adds greater rigidity to the structure.

The rail and two runners are then glued and screwed to the underside of the top shelf, and the same arrangement copied on the upper surface of the bottom panel, the runners commencing from a point immediately forward of the backing panel grooves.

Two 32mm (1¼in) No. 6 countersunk woodscrews are sufficient to secure each drawer rail in place, but the runners require three screws each to prevent the boards, or the runners themselves, bending slightly as the wood inevitably dries, the former being the more likely. Wood glue adds considerably to the strength of each rail and runner assembly.

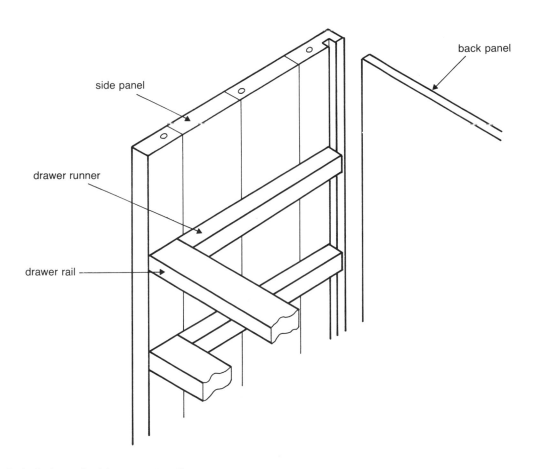

side panel

back panel

drawer runner

drawer rail

Exploded view of cabinet construction.

Fasten the drawer rail and two runners to the top side of the bottom panel with wood glue and screws.

Measure the positions of the two intermediate drawer runners on the inside faces of the two sides, leaving enough clearance for the two drawer rails to be fitted at the front. Check also that the marked positions are identical for both side panels so that the drawers will be perfectly level, and glue and screw these runners in place.

The side panels are attached to the top shelf and bottom panel with dowel joints as are the drawer rails fitted to the sides. Each joint between a side and the top or bottom panel requires three dowels, measured and spaced evenly apart. The drawer rails, however, only need a single dowel for each joint with the two sides because the rear edge of the rail butts tightly up against the forward end of the runners, resisting any tendency to rotate.

As the dowel positions must be marked in very precisely between the side panels and the top shelf and bottom panel, it is advisable to make a simple template from a strip of wood measuring 19 × 19mm ($\frac{3}{4}$ × $\frac{3}{4}$in) in cross-section and 390mm (15$\frac{3}{8}$in) in length, this being exactly equal to the width of both sides. Carefully measure and mark the positions of the three dowels along its length, drilling through the 19mm ($\frac{3}{4}$in) thickness of the wooden template with a 2mm ($\frac{3}{32}$in) diameter twist drill, thereby providing three holes through which a 25mm (1in) panel pin can be passed to mark the dowel positions on the boards.

If you are wondering why it is necessary to go to such elaborate lengths with a template, you will see the benefit of it when marking the pin-point positions

Each side panel has two drawer runners glued and screwed in place, and the drawer rails attached with dowels.

because as the template is equal in thickness to that of the side panels, it can be placed precisely on their end-grains, its edges flush with their sides; and to mark the top shelf and bottom panel, it need simply be laid up against the drawer runners, as the sides will be eventually.

Tap the head of the panel pin lightly with a small hammer to make a series of tiny impressions, and then place the tip of the 6mm ($\frac{1}{4}$in) diameter auger bit in each indentation and drill out the holes. The top shelf and bottom panel should be laid flat on the workbench and the holes drilled to a depth of approximately 16mm ($\frac{5}{8}$in), which will be just short of the point where the tip of the auger bit breaks through on the opposite side of the wood. It is not necessary to have assembled the ledge to the top shelf yet, but if you have already joined the parts

together, the projecting ledge can merely be hung over the end of the workbench out of the way.

Clamp the side panels in the workbench vice (some additional means of support may be required) and drill the dowel holes into the end-grain to a depth of 25mm (1in).

Determine the positions of the dowel-holes needed to join the drawer rails to the side panels, and drill these likewise, taking the same care not to bore right through the sides, and drilling deeper into the end-grain of the rails.

Cut the strip of 6mm ($\frac{1}{4}$in) diameter dowelling into sixteen lengths, each measuring 38mm ($1\frac{1}{2}$in), chamfer the ends lightly by giving a few twists in a pencil sharpener and cut a shallow glue channel along the length of each dowel with the tenon saw.

The top shelf is fitted in place to complete the main assembly of the cabinet.

Mix a quantity of wood glue and begin by joining the two intermediate drawer rails to the two sides. Then assemble the two sides to the bottom panel, and slide the plywood backing panel down into its housing grooves. Finally, join the top shelf to the sides to complete the assembly, knocking all the joints down into place by tapping with the mallet and a piece of clean scrap wood.

If it is not possible to cramp the cabinet together while the glue dries and sets hard, apply downward pressure on the top shelf by arranging heavy weights evenly upon its surface, protecting the wood with old newspapers.

Cut the feet from 45×19mm ($1\frac{3}{4} \times \frac{3}{4}$in) material, marking the curved pattern from a cut-out card template in order to provide a uniform appearance. The corners are mitred, so it is best to cut each piece to length in the mitre-box using the tenon saw.

When the main cabinet assembly is completed, turn it upside-down on the workbench and glue the feet in position, two in each corner, their outer faces flush with the edges of the bottom panel, and strengthen the mitre joints with 25mm (1in) panel pins. Once the glue has set hard, sandpaper the cabinet with medium and then fine-grade paper, always working in the direction of the grain.

Now for the three drawers, which should all be of the same size, provided you have measured correctly the positions of the intermediate drawer rails and runners. If there are any slight differ-

The feet are attached in pairs at each corner of the cabinet, on the underside of
the bottom panel, their ends mitred for a neat finish.

ences, you will simply have to make minor alterations to the overall dimensions of each drawer, and rely on your own measurements rather than those quoted in the cutting list, which serve as a guide only.

Taking the drawers one at a time, begin by cutting the front panel to size. Start by measuring the width of the drawer opening, subtracting 2mm ($\frac{3}{32}$in) at each end – to prevent the finished drawer from fitting too tightly – then square all around and cut with the tenon saw. Cut the rear panel to exactly the same size. Measure the two side panels to length, noting that allowance must be made for the pins of the dovetail joints used in the drawer construction.

The front panel is now given an edging profile identical to that applied on the three edges of the top shelf and bottom panel. Fit the corner-round cutter back in the router and, with the drawer front firmly clamped to the workbench, make a cut across both end-grains before finishing with a matching cut along the top and bottom edges, working the router all the time on the outside surface of the panel.

We now come to the dovetail joints. Do not be put off by the need for this type of joint, because although the dovetail always looks rather complicated, there is really not much more difficulty in preparing it provided that you mark the pins and the slots accurately. For that

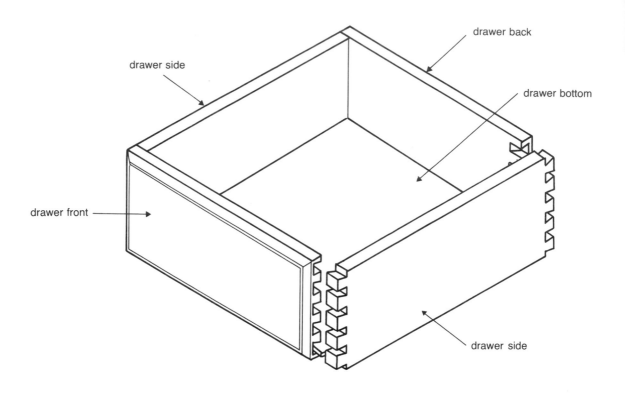

drawer back

drawer bottom

drawer side

drawer front

drawer side

Exploded view of drawer construction.

reason, it is a good idea to prepare a template from a piece of card so that you can be sure of consistency between all the joints. The number of dovetails per joint is up to you, but for this size of drawer, four or five equally spaced pins would seem a suitable number.

As the joints are to remain out of sight when each drawer is in the closed position, lapped dovetails are required in which the pins do not pass right through the thickness of either the drawer front or the rear panel. This needs much greater care in the sawing and chiselling of the slots, although the preparation can be simplified and speeded up by using a special dovetail jig in which the pins

and slots are lined up accurately and machined with a power-drill attachment.

Whatever method you choose, cut all the joints but do not attempt to fit them together as a test, because it can be very difficult if not impossible to separate them again without damaging the dovetail pins. Instead, it is preferable to line one part of the joint up against the other and make a visual comparison to judge whether the two parts will fit easily together, trimming where necessary.

Cut a groove for the bottom panel of the drawer on the inside face of each drawer component, using the router fitted with the same 6mm ($\frac{1}{4}$in) diameter straight cutter as was employed for the preparation of the housing grooves in the four main panels of the cabinet. The drawer groove should be set 9mm ($\frac{3}{8}$in) up from the bottom edge and cut to a depth of approximately 6mm ($\frac{1}{4}$in). Cut it along the full length of the two drawer sides, but stop it fractionally short of the ends of the front and back panels.

Measure and cut the bottom panel from the sheet of 6mm ($\frac{1}{4}$in) thick plywood, allowing the extra amounts that fit into the grooves. Mix some wood glue, apply it with a small brush to the joints and begin by assembling the front and back panels to one of the sides. Then slide the drawer bottom into its grooves and finally attach the second side, knocking all the dovetails fully home with the mallet and a block of clean scrap wood before cramping up the assembly. Wipe away all traces of surplus wood glue with a damp cloth.

When the glue has hardened completely, remove the cramps and rub down with fine-grade sandpaper to remove all remaining traces of glue from the surfaces of the joints. Test the drawer to see that it fits properly into the cabinet.

You can choose from a wide range of drawer knobs and handles made from a variety of materials, but brass probably gives the best finish. Measure the position where you want to fit the handle on the drawer front, and drill out the holes

Fitting a drawer handle.

with a small twist drill. Apply the desired finish to the cabinet and its three drawers, and attach the handles.

The drawers will slide more easily in and out on their runners if a little wax polish is rubbed along the upper edges of the runners and the bottom edges of the drawer sides.

You could adapt the dimensions of this simple three-drawer bedside cabinet to build a matching chest of drawers or dressing-table.

CHAPTER SIX

KITCHEN TABLE

The pine kitchen table is one of those items of furniture which can so easily be adapted to the requirements of the household and, indeed, to the size of the kitchen, simply by increasing or decreasing its dimensions. For while its height will remain constant, the general shape of the table may take on the form of a square or a rectangle, or even a circle if so desired, with only slight adjustments made to the length of the rails, and the length and width of the table top. In all instances, the four legs stay the same.

Other variations are possible: for example, the illustrated table has plain rails, but you could add a drawer at each end to make for a more versatile piece of kitchen furniture.

So the first matter to consider is size: how many people are regularly going to use the table, and how much space is available to accommodate it? As a rough guide, our table will seat up to six people and would require quite a large kitchen to provide sufficient room for the chairs.

As for the table itself, it is traditional in its method of construction, using mortise and tenon joints to attach the rails to the legs, the table top being made up from numerous narrow strips of wood butted tightly together and glued into a single board which is fixed to the frame of the table with wooden joining blocks.

Cutting List

Leg: four of 698 × 63 × 63mm
        ($27\frac{1}{2}$ × $2\frac{1}{2}$ × $2\frac{1}{2}$in)
Long rail: two of 1220 × 120 × 19mm
        (48 × $4\frac{3}{4}$ × $\frac{3}{4}$in)
Short rail: two of 662 × 120 × 19mm
        ($26\frac{1}{16}$ × $4\frac{3}{4}$ × $\frac{3}{4}$in)
Table top: seventeen of 1320 × 45 × 32mm
        (52 × $1\frac{3}{4}$ × $1\frac{1}{4}$in)

The first stage is to make the four legs, and this will need some experience of wood-turning and access to a lathe. The general principles of wood-turning have already been discussed elsewhere in the book, and it is sufficient to say that, although the preparation of the legs may appear rather complicated, this is not, in fact, the case; provided you have facilities for turning wood, the task of turning and shaping the legs is no more difficult than making the components of a stool or chair, except that the table legs are quite a bit larger and heavier.

Once again, a full-sized lathe is ideal if you have one, but a small worktop lathe will be able to cope; although you must expect less powerful models to have a reduced capacity for turning at a very high speed. The length and weight of the wood should also prompt you to increase

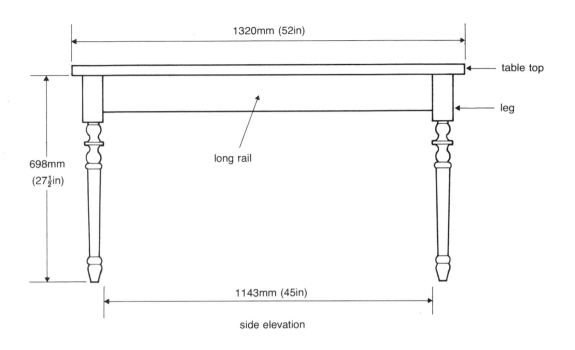

1320mm (52in)

table top

leg

long rail

698mm
($27\frac{1}{2}$in)

1143mm (45in)

side elevation

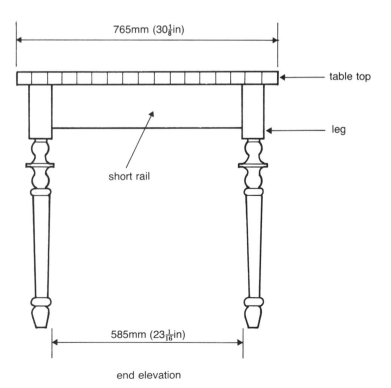

765mm ($30\frac{1}{8}$in)

table top

leg

short rail

585mm ($23\frac{1}{16}$in)

end elevation

Main dimensions of the kitchen table.

your safety precautions, in the possible event of the workpiece becoming detached accidentally from the lathe as it is rotating. Safety goggles are *always* needed for the eyes and ear protectors are desirable to safeguard the hearing from prolonged exposure to high-pitched machinery. Use thick gloves to shield the fingers, at the expense of some loss in manual dexterity, and a padded jacket or overall, completing the ensemble with a hat or helmet. If these precautions seem unduly elaborate, you will certainly change your opinion after witnessing the first piece of wood 'slipping' out of the lathe – so be prepared.

Before commencing with the turning of the four table legs, make a rough sketch of how you want the finished legs to look. Usually the top portion retains its square cross-section, as this is the part that will have mortises cut in it to receive the tenons at the ends of the rails, and in length it is somewhat greater than the width of the rails. From the point at which the turning begins, the pattern is partly a matter of convention, partly personal choice. Normally, the upper part of the turning involves some intricate detail, but remains solidly bulbous, followed by a gradual tapering down of a column to the foot of the leg, which once again assumes a decoratively curved configuration.

Decide upon the required proportions and clearly mark these on the plan so that they may be quickly and accurately transferred on to the material and mounted in the lathe. This will ensure a high degree of consistency between the four legs, each of the major sections being measured and pencilled in with a heavy line which will be easy to see when the wood is rotated at high speed.

Naturally, as each leg is shaped in turn, there will inevitably be some minor difference between one and another, and this is impossible to avoid. As a matter of fact, it could be argued that small variations in the way each leg is turned adds to the individuality of the finished piece. Taken to its logical conclusion, you might even wish to make all the legs slightly differently as part of the design.

The four legs are turned from material measuring 63×63mm ($2\frac{1}{2} \times 2\frac{1}{2}$in) in cross-section and 760mm ($29\frac{7}{8}$in) in length, the finished length of the legs being 698mm ($27\frac{1}{2}$in) (when turning wood it is usual to work with a piece that is longer than needed, the ends being trimmed upon completion of the lathe work).

Starting with the first leg, cut both ends perfectly square and mark the exact centre of each end-grain by drawing two straight pencil lines between diagonal corners, the centre being the point where the two lines cross. Mount the material between the headstock and tailstock of the lathe, setting the tool-rest in such a position that the leg can be rotated without any of the four corners coming into contact with it, but allowing a small clearance. Set the lathe briefly in motion to check that it runs up to full speed, free from vibration, and then stop it again.

At the headstock end measure off 178mm (7in), of which 25mm (1in) is accounted for by the waste at the end which will eventually be removed, and 152mm (6in) – the uppermost part of the leg to which the rails will be attached – all of which will remain square in cross-section. At this point, make a clear pencil mark and then, setting the lathe in motion again, commence the process of turning the rest of the leg into a cylinder, cutting the corners back with the spindle

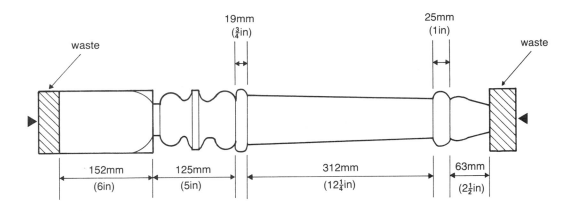

19mm
($\frac{3}{4}$in)

25mm
(1in)

waste

waste

152mm
(6in)

125mm
(5in)

312mm
(12$\frac{1}{4}$in)

63mm
(2$\frac{1}{2}$in)

Main dimensions of the table legs.

gouge and parting tool. It is sufficient at the moment simply to produce a perfectly round surface, in which the maximum amount of waste is removed from the four corners, with the minimum reduction from the point halfway across the width and thickness of the material, thus providing a cylinder with parallel sides with which to begin the task of shaping the curved and tapered sections.

We have already established that the top part of the leg – the section which is not subject to turning – measures 152mm (6in) in length, and the next step is to measure the other three successive sections: 140mm (5½in) for the intricately curved stage, 328mm (12⅞in) for the tapered part of the leg and 80mm (3⅛in) for the foot. Once again, mark in these divisions in thick pencil, set the wood turning and cut into the marked lines with the parting tool to create a series of easily identified sections. The order in which you carry out the turning and, indeed, the shaping of the foot and the decorative curves, is a matter of individual choice.

However, it is wise to remember that

redwood is a particularly fibrous softwood with a large grain, and if you attempt to work too vigorously with the various wood-turning tools, damage can easily be inflicted on the surface – so proceed carefully, applying gentle pressure to the tools and pausing often to survey the result. As the shaping of the leg nears its conclusion, employ smaller gouges to accentuate the various divisions and grooves. Finally, sandpaper the spinning leg with medium and then fine-grade paper to produce a perfect, smooth surface.

Remove the first leg from the lathe, and use it as a pattern for the other three legs, following precisely the same method in each case. This time, you are effectively copying instead of creating, and the varying diameters along the different sections can be checked using a pair of geometrical dividers or micrometer callipers, measuring the relevant part of the first leg and turning the other legs to match.

When all the legs have been prepared satisfactorily, square a line around the four flat faces, 25mm (1in) from the top

Create the initial shaping of the leg with the spindle gouge and parting tool, before changing to smaller gouges for more intricate detail.

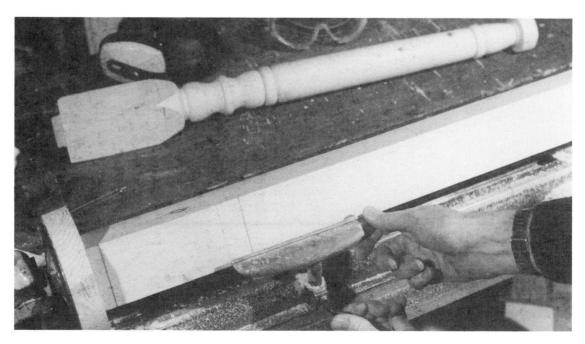

As a piece of wood for one of the legs is attached to the lathe, the first leg can be seen on the workbench, serving as a pattern.

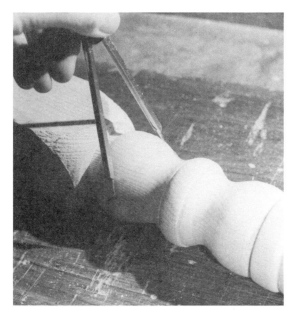

Check the diameter of all the turned parts of the leg with a pair of dividers or callipers to ensure consistency between all four legs.

end, and remove the waste with the tenon saw. Also remove the small amount of excess wood immediately below the turned foot. All the legs should now measure 698mm (27½in) in length.

The next step is to join the rails to the legs, using mortise and tenon joints. For maximum strength, the mortises should be cut as deeply as possible, which means that two mortises, each one being made in an adjacent edge, will overlap within the wood. The ends of the tenons must, therefore, be mitred, thus permitting them to meet at right-angles.

As the rails measure 19mm (¾in) in thickness, the mortises should be set to a width of 13mm (½in), which will retain sufficient strength in the thickness of the tenon while giving two shoulders, each measuring 3mm (⅛in) deep. Set the two pointers of the mortise gauge to a gap of

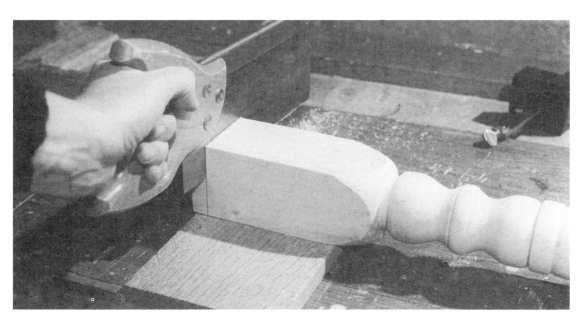

Measure the top end of the leg to its correct length, square around the piece and remove the unwanted excess portion with the tenon saw.

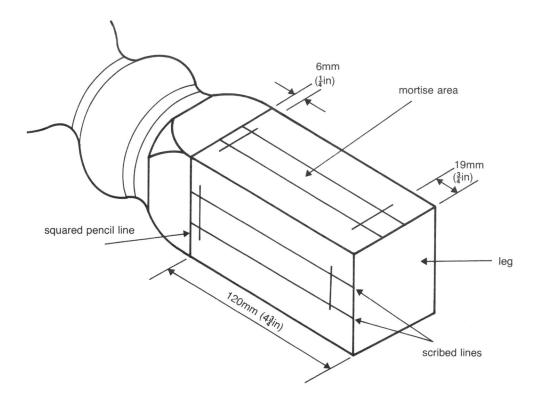

Marking in the mortise position for each leg.

13mm (½in) and adjust the fence so that the spurs scribe each face centrally. The top of the leg measures 63mm (2½in) wide and 63mm (2½in) thick, so once the gauge is set correctly for one edge it will also be correct for the adjacent side.

Examine the leg carefully, and if there are any slight imperfections in the woodturning, or in the appearance of some knots which might be better concealed on the inside of the table, choose the two surfaces which seem best suited to having mortises marked and cut in them. Scribe a pair of parallel lines on each face with the mortise gauge, marking to a length of 120mm (4¾in) from the top end,

this being equal to the width of the rails. Set in each mortise by 19mm (¾in) from the top and 6mm (¼in) from the bottom.

Clamp the leg horizontally in the workbench vice, and prepare the mortise by firstly drilling out most of the waste with a 13mm (½in) diameter twist drill or auger bit mounted in the handbrace, boring a series of holes along the marked-out area to a depth of 38mm (1½in). The depth can easily be determined by wrapping some sticky tape around the shaft of the drill bit. Having completed the drilling in one mortise, turn the leg through 90 degrees to bring the second marked-out mortise into view, and drill another

Remove the bulk of the waste from the mortise by drilling a series of holes with a 13mm ($\frac{1}{2}$in) diameter centre bit.

series of holes into the wood until they break through into the first row of holes. Each time a hole is drilled, make sure that the drill bit works within the scribed mortise lines – as the mortise measures 13mm ($\frac{1}{2}$in) wide, and the drill is of 13mm ($\frac{1}{2}$in) diameter, there is no room for error.

Remove the leg from the vice and shake out all the small bits of wood from the holes. Then clamp it firmly again and chop out the rest of the waste with a 13mm ($\frac{1}{2}$in) chisel and mallet, cutting clean straight sides and ends to each of the pair of mortises, continually checking that they both correspond exactly with one another. Repeat the same procedure with the other three legs.

Having completed the mortises, the next stage is to cut the tenons in the four rails. Up to now, you could have kept an

Complete the preparation of the mortise by chopping out the remaining waste with the chisel and mallet.

open mind about the shape and size of the table, but the preparation of the rails will determine the proportions of the table, whether the frame is to be a square or a rectangle, and how large it will be. If you were to opt for a square table, all the rails would be of the same length, but a rectangular table requires two long and two short rails. Assuming the latter, measure and mark the two long rails, allowing an extra 38mm (1½in) at each end for the tenon, square around the material and cut the rails equally to length.

The tenon is prepared in the following way. Begin by measuring and marking the depth of the tenon, this being 38mm (1½in) from the end of the wood, and square a line all around the rail in pencil. Take the mortise gauge and, retaining the same gap between the two spurs as was used for marking in the mortises, adjust the fence so that the pointers are set halfway across the 19mm (¾in) thickness of the rail. Scribe the shoulder lines for the tenon along the two edges and the end-grain of the rail. It is good practice to mark in the tenon at the other end of the rail at the same time, working the fence of the mortise gauge against the same side of the material to minimize errors.

Clamp the rail in the workbench vice at an angle approximating to 45 degrees, and carefully saw down on the waste side of both the scribed markings using the tenon saw. Cut down as far as the squared pencil line, and then turn the piece over in the vice and repeat the same procedure from the opposite edge. Finally, set the rail upright and saw down to the depth line.

Remove the rail from the vice, secure it to the end of the workbench with clamps, or lay it flat on the bench-hook,

and cut down on the waste side of the squared pencil lines denoting the depth of the tenon until the portions of unwanted wood are removed. It is often necessary to clean up the inside corners of the shoulders with the chisel to cut away small pieces of wood that the tenon saw did not quite reach.

Set in the second pair of shoulders – by 19mm (¾in) at the top of the rail, and 6mm (¼in) at the bottom – to match the setting in of the mortise, mark these accurately with the square and pencil and remove the waste with the tenon saw.

Make a trial fitting of the joint. If both parts have been measured and cut with accuracy, the tenon should tap into the mortise with gently applied pressure from the mallet until it fits fully home. However, if you view the joint through the mortise cut in the adjacent side, you will see that the tenon effectively blocks the path of the tenon that will be cut in the other neighbouring rail. The only way for both tenons to be accommodated is to cut a mitre at the end of each one.

A rough-and-ready way to mark in the mitre is simply to run a pencil down inside the adjacent mortise, when the tenon is fully in position, on the innermost side, remove the rail from the leg, hold the rail level on the workbench and saw down between the pencil line and the corner end of the tenon, thus trimming off a triangular block of waste. When the same is done to the tenon on the other rail, fitting into the second mortise, the two mitres should permit the ends of the tenons to meet perfectly.

A more precise way of marking in the mitres at the end of the tenons is to use a mitre-square, where the blade of the square is set at an angle of 45 degrees to the handle. This will enable you to mark

Fit the tenon into its mortise, and mark in the line of the mitre by inserting a pencil through the adjacent mortise.

Cut the mitre at the end of the tenon with the tenon saw.

When all of the tenons have had mitres cut at their ends, each rail will fit fully up against the leg.

the required mitre angles on the top and bottom shoulders of the tenon, joining them up with a pencilled line on one of the main shoulders, and cutting off the waste, as before, with the tenon saw. Either way, some further trimming of the tenons may be necessary before both adjacent rails fit properly to each leg.

There is one additional matter to consider with respect to all four rails before they are fitted to the legs and their tenons mitred: you should carefully examine their surfaces to check for any imperfections, unsightly or awkward knots, small splits in the grain, or some such similar fault, so that the better of the two surfaces faces outwards, with all irregularities kept out of sight by being on the inside.

When the mortise and tenon joints are completed, and the rails fit perfectly to the legs, mix a quantity of wood glue and apply it by brush to each of the joints, assembling the framework of the table. Commence with the two ends, comprising the two shorter rails each joined to two legs, thus forming a pair of sub-assemblies, and then join the two longer rails, firstly to one of these sub-assemblies, and finally adding the second sub-assembly to complete the frame. Stand it on a level surface and check that all the legs stand in correct alignment with each other, and that none of them is splayed inwards or outwards. Allow sufficient time for the glue to set completely.

The next stage is to construct the table top. Strictly speaking, you can decide for yourself whether you want the top to be made up of a large number of narrow strips of wood, or a small number of wide boards. In the illustrated table, seventeen lengths of wood have been used, each measuring 45mm (1¾in) wide and 32mm (1¼in) thick, but it could just as easily have been eight lengths measuring 96mm (3¾in) wide and 32mm (1¼in) thick. The former arrangement is preferred because, in spite of the fact that it involves a great deal more joining together, the narrower widths to some extent simplify the construction of the table top since these are less inclined to warp.

First of all, cut each of the pieces of wood longer than the required length of the table top, to allow for the two ends to be squared and cut to the proper size once they have all been joined together. Now spend some time placing the pieces of wood in an order which provides an attractive distribution of knots, a realistic matching of the varying grain patterns and some consistency in overall tone. It should be possible to butt their edges tightly together and judge the effect of the table top as it will appear in its finished form.

When you are satisfied with the look of the composite top – after much trial and error, moving the strips around – mark their order 1 to 17, and then set them out on top of the workbench, laid on a sheet of newspaper, so that when they are all glued together, they do not adhere to the worktop. Mix a very large quantity of wood glue, for it is far better to make too much and waste some, rather than run out halfway through and have to pause to mix more; apply the glue to the abutting edges of the seventeen strips. Bring each one into contact, starting with the first and second pieces and continuing until the final strip has been joined.

It is not enough merely to place the strips in contact; they must be pressed tightly together while the glue dries, and normally cramps would be employed for

Arrange all the pieces of wood for the table top so that the knots are spread in a seemingly natural pattern.

this purpose. But the assembled board also needs to be kept absolutely flat, otherwise the table top will not rest properly on the table frame, so some additional support must be supplied. One answer, somewhat complicated in appearance, but very effective, is to obtain four sturdy pieces of metal, such as the L-shaped steel sections from old dismantled bedframes, and mount them in pairs at opposite ends of the assembly, one laid on top of the board and the other directly beneath it, clamping these together to keep the table top flat, while binding heavy string in three different positions to hold all of the individual strips in close contact, applying a tourniquet to each one to increase the pressure.

Place scrap blocks of wood between the string and the edges of the assembly, to prevent compression marks from being made on the two outermost strips – unless you know in advance that the finished board is too wide and will need to be planed down, in which case any marks will be removed.

When the glue has dried thoroughly, and after removing the contrivances used to press it together, lift the board carefully off the workbench and peel the newspaper from the underside.

It is quite possible that some of the wood strips making up the table top do not lie perfectly flat with their immediate neighbours, and so these slight irregularities in the surface will need to be

After gluing all the table top strips together, pressure is applied in the form of string or cord, tightened with tourniquets, and the assembled panel kept perfectly flat by mounting straight-edged steel bars in pairs, clamped together, one at each end.

Once the table top panel is complete and the glue has dried and hardened, both main surfaces are lightly planed and thoroughly sandpapered to produce a smooth flat finish.

smoothed out. Lightly plane down the board on both main surfaces, and then rub down thoroughly with medium and fine-grade sandpaper.

Measure the table top to its correct length and width. In determining its length, decide how much of an overhang you wish to project beyond the legs and the rails, noting that there should be some consistency between the amount projecting beyond the sides and the ends.

Mark the ends of the table top square and cut to the required length using the handsaw or jig-saw, and plane the end-grain. In this instance, the edges and ends of the table are kept square in pro-file, but you could round them off or produce a more decorative edge-moulding with the router and an appropriate cutter.

The table top is attached to the frame with joining blocks, a total of twelve blocks being used, two blocks mounted at each end of the frame and three blocks to each side. These may either be triangular wooden blocks, glued in position, or rectangular blocks fastened with screws. Each block should measure 100mm (4in) in length; for a triangular shape, cut from a length of 45 × 45mm (1¾ × 1¾in) softwood, sawn in half between diagonally opposite corners; or for a rectangular shape, cut to size from

The end-grain of the table top is planed square and flat, lengths of straight-edged scrap wood being clamped in position to act as a guide for the smoothing plane.

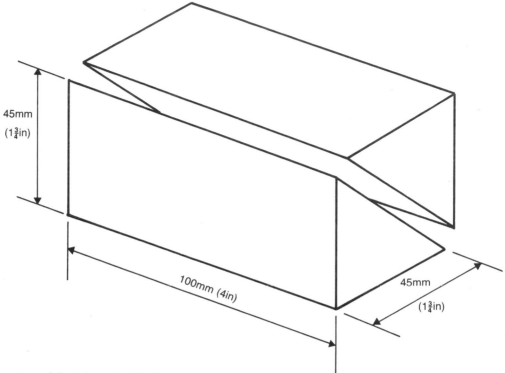

45mm
($1\frac{3}{4}$in)

100mm (4in)

45mm

($1\frac{3}{4}$in)

Dimensions of the triangular blocks.

The triangular-shaped wooden joining blocks are glued between the inside surface of the rails and the underside of the table top.

material measuring 32 × 32mm ($1\frac{1}{4}$ × $1\frac{1}{4}$in), or similar.

Lay the table top on the workbench, bottom side up, and place the table frame, also upside-down on the top, measuring and adjusting it until it is in exactly the required position. Apply glue or screws to the joining blocks and fix them between the underside of the table and the inside face of the four rails, spacing them regularly apart.

The table is now complete and only needs to be finished with several coats of varnish, or any other treatment that you wish to use.

THE KITCHEN TABLE WITH DRAWER

A kitchen table with a drawer at one or both ends is a variation that will appeal to households where storage facilities are limited, and in this case the provision of extra drawer space may seem an opportunity not to be missed.

Actually, the method of construction is not greatly complicated by the addition of drawers; indeed, much of the preparation remains the same. The turning of the legs is identical, as is the cutting of mortises and tenons for the two long rails to be attached, and the assembling of the composite table top. The difference is that where the drawer is to be fitted at one end, or both, the full-width rail is replaced by two shallower rails, referred to as the top rail and the drawer rail, each of which is cut from material measuring 42 × 19mm ($1\frac{5}{8}$ × $\frac{3}{4}$in). The top rail is dovetail-jointed to the legs so that its upper side lies flush with the end-grain of the legs. The drawer rail is fitted with mortise and tenon joints in such a position that its upper side is level with the bottom edge of the adjacent side rails.

Drawer runners are cut from 45 × 19mm ($1\frac{3}{4}$ × $\frac{3}{4}$in) material and fastened with nails to the bottom edge of the side rails, running their full length, providing support for the drawer or drawers.

The drawer is of standard construction, consisting of a drawer front and back panel, dovetail-jointed to the two side panels, all prepared from matching pine, and all of which have a groove cut along the lower inside face to receive a plywood bottom panel.

The drawer slides in between the top rail and the drawer rail, and drawer stops – small blocks of scrap wood – are glued to the inside faces of the side rails to prevent the drawer from being pushed in any further than the point where the drawer front is flush with the drawer rail. One or two knobs should be fitted to the drawer, and a lock could be included if you wish to secure its contents.

CHAPTER SEVEN

KITCHEN CHAIR

The kitchen chair is of such a basic shape that there is not a great deal that can be done to make for an original appearance except to alter the proportions, create slightly different decorative effects on the turned components, or change the shape of the seat and the backrest. Other than that, the layout remains the same. However, as with all handmade furniture, the individual character of the piece derives not so much from the pattern but from the minute detail, the marking and cutting of the seat curves, the shaping of the backrest, the working of the decoration on the spindles supporting the backrest, and so on.

Indeed, this principle holds true for most of the items in this book, and for many others to be found elsewhere, and often there is a preference to follow a well-known design, something solid and traditional, rather than opt for a piece of artistic impracticality.

The kitchen chair is a logical progression from the stool, although it differs in several respects. Inevitably it involves quite a lot of wood-turning, so once again you will need access to a lathe of some description. This could be either a full-sized workshop lathe, which is the most versatile and dependable sort, or a lightweight workbench lathe, capable of producing excellent results but with less

---

Cutting List

Seat: four of 400 × 95 × 32mm
(15¾ × 3¾ × 1¼in)
Backrest: one of 508 × 150 × 75mm
(20 × 6 × 3in)
Leg: four of 439 × 45mm (17¼ × 1¾in)
diameter mopstick
Backrest spindle: six of 255 × 32 × 32mm
(10 × 1¼ × 1¼in)
Leg rail: three of 340 × 32 × 32mm
(13⅜ × 1¼ × 1¼in)

---

capacity, or a workbench-mounted lathe accessory powered by an ordinary electric drill which, for its size and expense, is a remarkably reliable choice.

Of course, the first example is not something you would rush out and purchase simply because you want to make a set of kitchen chairs, but the other two alternatives certainly bring wood-turning into the realms of possibility for most keen woodworkers, and once you have acquired the skill of spinning a length of pine into a finely shaped leg or spindle, you are sure to pursue the craft with even more enthusiasm.

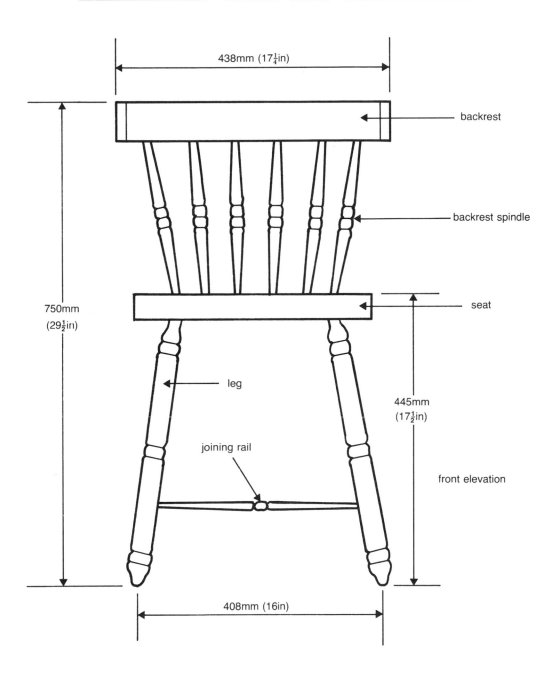

Main dimensions of the kitchen chair.

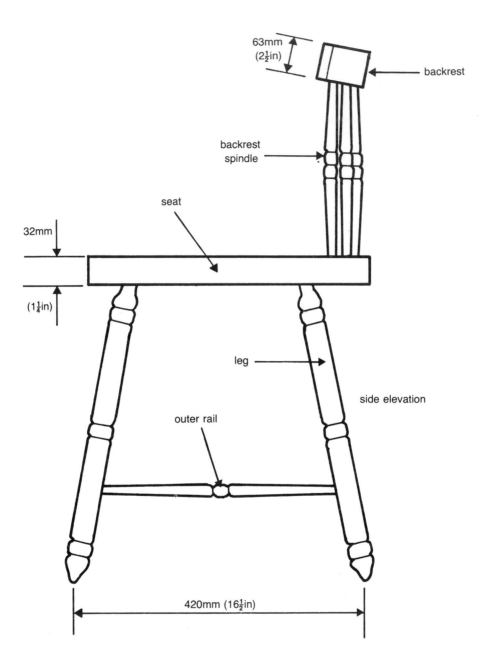

63mm
(2½in)

backrest

backrest
spindle

seat

32mm

(1¼in)

leg

side elevation

outer rail

420mm (16½in)

Main dimensions – side view.

The making of the kitchen chair entails three separate stages before all of the parts are ready for assembly. The first of these is the preparation of the seat, followed by the cutting and shaping of the curved backrest, and then the turning of the four legs, six backrest spindles and three leg rails.

We will begin with the seat. Its overall dimensions before marking in and cutting the curved edges, are 400mm (15¾in) long and 380mm (15in) wide in the form of a rectangle, its thickness being 32mm (1¼in). As pine boards are not supplied in widths of 380mm (15in), clearly the seat will have to be constructed from several narrower sections, and in this instance it is made from four pieces each measuring 95 × 32mm (3¾ × 1¼in) in cross-section and 400mm (15¾in) in length. It would be equally feasible to make up the seat from fewer boards of greater width, or more boards of lesser width.

However, there is one additional consideration, and that is the thickness of the seat. When you purchase wood from the timber supplier, the standard thicknesses after planing are 19mm (¾in) and 45mm (1¾in), the former being too little, and the latter too great. If the supplier has facilities for planing timber, simply ask for a plank measuring 45mm (1¾in) thick to be reduced to 32mm (1¼in), and the task will take only a few minutes. Should you buy your material from a DIY store with no such facility, you may be able to enlist the help of a local joinery for a small consideration, or plane down the wood yourself using an electric planer.

Arrange the four separate pieces on the top of the workbench so that the knots which will inevitably be present

Set the four lengths of wood for the seat side by side so that the knots are realistically distributed, and check that the edges can be butted tightly up against each other.

are distributed evenly and to your own taste, and check that the adjoining edges can all be butted tightly up against each other without showing any gaps. Sometimes it is necessary to shift the pieces around before you come up with an acceptable combination, for while it is important to be satisfied with the appearance of the composite panel – not having all the knots on one side, for example – it is even more important to ensure that the butt-jointed edges all fit perfectly in complete contact, otherwise the strength of the seat could be compromised.

Mix a quantity of wood glue, and apply it thoroughly to each of the abutting edge surfaces, bringing them into contact with one another on a flat surface. The joints must be kept under pressure while the glue dries and sets hard, and the usual method is to apply two sash-cramps and tightened them up to exert the required force. Each cramp has a long straight-edged beam, and the assembled seat will rest on this to keep the board absolutely flat.

If you do not possess cramps and feel that you cannot justify their expense, an alternative technique is to tie two pieces of very strong cord or string around the assembly, in much the same position as the cramps would be placed, and apply a tourniquet to each one so that it can be tightened to a very high tension. Two flat-edged pieces of wood can be laid beneath the seat to ensure perfect flatness, with a sheet of newspaper placed between these and the underside of the assembled boards to prevent the glue that squeezes out from inadvertently sticking them together!

The disadvantage of employing this method instead of the proper clamps is not because of any reduced pressure exerted on the assembly, but is due to the fact that the string cuts into the outermost edges of the wood and leaves indentations afterwards. But this may be obviated by inserting small scrap wood blocks and, in any case, the edges will be cut later when the seat is prepared to the desired shape and size.

When the glue has set completely, after at least a day, take off the cramps, or unbind the tourniquets and peel away the newspaper, some of which will have adhered to the surface of the seat. Where glue has squeezed out from the joins and hardened, this should be carefully removed with a sharp chisel, and both the top and bottom surfaces planed lightly and then rubbed down with sandpaper to produce a clean, smooth finish.

Now we come to the marking out of the seat on the rectangular board. Essentially, the side and front edges are given only a slight degree of curvature, with nicely rounded front corners, whereas the rear edge has a circular arc described upon it with a pencil and compass. Although the curves for the sides and the front can be drawn freehand, there is always the danger of inconsistency between one side and the other, and you are advised to use either artist's curves or some alternative guide such as the edge of a tray or anything else that will produce the required result.

Note that if you have constructed the seat panel from four separate boards, there will be a line running down the centre of the rectangle – barely visible, if you have jointed the boards tightly together, but still noticeable – about which both halves of the seat should be symmetrical. This faint line serves as a position for the pivot of the compasses employed to draw the circular arc at the

The bedside cabinet (Chapter 5).

The single bed (Chapter 10).

The kitchen table and chair (Chapters 6 and 7).

The stool (Chapter 3).

The kitchen preparation trolley (Chapter 9).

The bathroom cabinet (Chapter 4).

The corner cabinet (Chapter 8).

The bookcase shelving unit (Chapter 1).

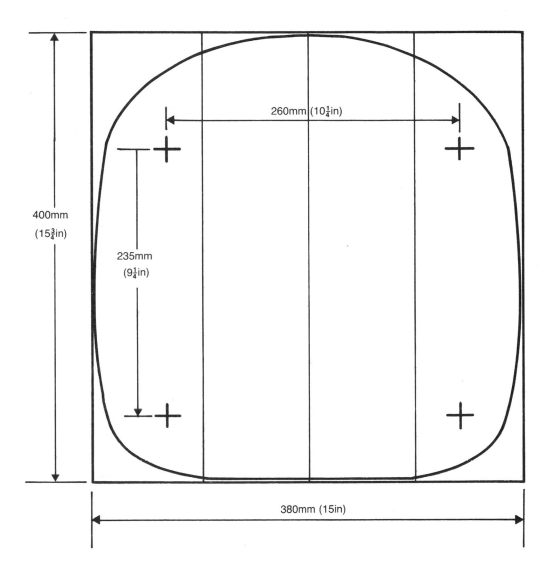

Position of the holes for the legs.

rear of the seat. Ordinary geometrical compasses are too small, and you can either make your own enlarged version from two pieces of hinged wood, with a pencil fastened at the end of one, and a thin pointed pin at the end of the other, or else tie a length of string to the pencil and alter the length of it by trial and error until you arrive at the most appropriate radius, drawing in the curved line between the sides.

Fasten the seat at the end of the workbench with clamps and small blocks of scrap wood, to protect the surface of the seat, and gradually cut around the pencil line with the electric jig-saw, to which a

The pencil and string method may seem rudimentary, but it is an effective way of drawing an arc for the rear of the seat.

Cut around the marked outline of the seat with the jig-saw.

fine-cutting blade has been attached. The seat will need to be repositioned several times before the saw-blade can travel completely around the perimeter of the seat, and you may find that the waste comes away in stages, especially if the pencil lines are close to the edge of the board. Work the jig-saw with a firm guiding hand to ensure that it does not wander off course, otherwise you will spoil the appearance of the seat. Of course, some remedial action can be taken with the spokeshave to restore curves that have wobbled a little, and indeed this tool should be used to smooth down the edge, clamping the seat securely in the vice for this purpose before finishing with medium and fine-grade sandpaper.

Finally, rub down the corners between the edge and the top and bottom surfaces, paying particular attention to the upper side, rounding it off well towards the front of the seat.

The curved backrest should be prepared next. This will require a fairly large block of wood within which the shape of the backrest can be mapped out and cut. The block need only be sawn wood, since there will be a lot of sawing and planing before the backrest is completed. In this example, the shape is marked out on a block measuring 150×75mm (6×3in) in cross-section and approximately 508mm (20in) in length, providing a surplus at each end which will be trimmed to size later. The curvature of the backrest should be less pronounced than that for the rear of the seat, but the seat serves as a convenient pattern from which to begin.

Although the block of wood upon which the backrest is to be marked out has been obtained sawn rather than planed, thus saving some unnecessary expense, you will find that preparation of the piece will be made much easier if the two main surfaces of the block are planed either with the electric planer or the smoothing plane.

Place the completed seat on the upper surface of the block, and pencil around the curve, setting it so that at no point does the curve come nearer to the edge of

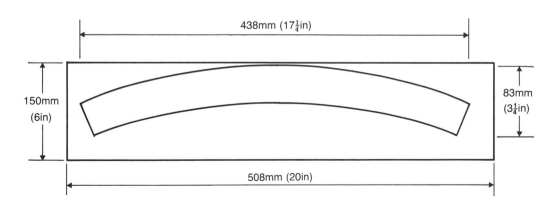

The curvature of the backrest.

When marking out the backrest, the seat curvature serves as an initial guide before
the pencil and string method is employed to increase the radius of curvature.

Cut roughly around the drawn shape of
the backrest with the jig-saw to remove
most of the waste.

the block than 25mm (1in) or so. Now re-attach the string to the pencil or use the home-made compasses, to draw a line of lesser curvature – which means a larger radius – so that it coincides with the rearmost position of the first curve, to produce a shallower line to represent the rear edge of the backrest. You must judge for yourself just how shallow or pronounced this curve ought to be but, for guidance, try to make it approximately halfway between the curve of the seat and the straight line of the block's rear edge.

Keeping to the same pivot point, pencil in a second curved line 32mm (1¼in) forward of the shallow backrest curve to delineate its front edge, continuing the line to the two ends of the block.

The most effective way of removing the large portions of unwanted waste from both sides of the two curved lines is to cut around them with the electric jig-saw fitted with a blade long enough to pass right through the thickness of the block. Clamp the material securely at the edge of the workbench, and work the saw-blade on the waste side of each line.

Allow the saw to progress slowly through the wood rather than attempting to exert too much pressure on the tool, as the thickness of the block inevitably provides resistance.

Actually, the jig-saw can still be used even if the saw-blade is slightly shorter than the block thickness, because it will cut equally well, the only problem being

that the waste will not come away as there is part of the thickness left uncut. However, this can quickly be finished off with the coping saw.

The backrest in this crudely cut form must now be fashioned to a more refined shape by clamping the piece in the vice and planing the inside and outside curves with the spokeshave. Any irregularities in the original cutting out can now be removed, and the surfaces of the backrest smoothed into clean, flowing curves. The ends, which so far have been left too long, can now be measured to length, a pencil line squared around each, and the waste trimmed away with the tenon saw. The top and bottom edges may need further planing to reduce

The outer curve of the backrest is planed with the spokeshave before all of the waste has been removed.

The inner curve is smoothed with the spokeshave, and the backrest gradually takes on the desired shape.

slightly the width of the backrest and to remove any indentations or marks that may have been caused by the cutting out process.

Use a coarse-to-medium grade sandpaper to rub down the corners of the piece, particularly that between the front surface and the top edge so that when it takes its place in the final chair assembly, the backrest will be comfortable to lean against. Once again, this part of the preparation lends itself to individual interpretation.

The last stage of the work is to make the four legs, six backrest spindles and three leg rails, all of which conform to a pattern. Actually, the wood-turning is quite straightforward, because all of the components consist initially of a long

cylindrical shape which is divided up into segments, decorated with little 'bobbins' every so often along each of the four legs, or positioned centrally along the spindles and leg rails.

Starting with the four legs, each of these is turned from a length of softwood mopstick, which is sold by most timber merchants as handrail material already turned into a near-perfect circle, with a slightly flattened edge, measuring approximately 45mm (1¾in) in diameter. The advantage of using this, of course, is that the initial process of turning square-section wood into a cylindrical shape is almost entirely done away with. All you have to do is measure in the centre of each end-grain, possibly using a template, and mount the mopstick in the lathe,

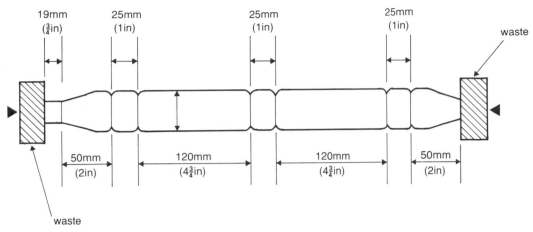

19mm (¾in)   25mm (1in)   25mm (1in)   25mm (1in)   waste

50mm (2in)   120mm (4¾in)   120mm (4¾in)   50mm (2in)

waste

Main dimensions of the chair legs.

ready for the leg pattern to be measured and marked along its length.

If you cannot find any suitable mopstick material, then you may resort to using lengths of 45 × 45mm (1¾ × 1¾in) softwood. Find the centre of each endgrain by drawing two straight lines between diagonally opposed corners, and mount likewise in the lathe.

The first stage in the wood-turning will then be to remove the four corners using the parting tool and the spindle gouge until the wood has been roughed into the shape of a cylinder.

The material for the leg is first turned in the lathe and worked with the spindle gouge to produce a perfect cylinder.

Either way, regardless of whether you start off with a mopstick or square-section wood, each piece must be cut somewhat longer than the length of the finished leg, to allow sufficient material for the joint at the top end and the 'casting off' at the end of the foot. The length of the finished leg measuring 420mm (16½in) from the bottom of the seat to the ground suggests that an overall length of 508mm (20in) is more than enough.

Make sure that you take the usual precautions: protecting your eyes from flying wood splinters by wearing goggles, with a respirator over the nose and mouth so that you do not inhale particles of fine dust, and ear-muffs to deaden the noise of the lathe.

Turn the wood to a diameter slightly greater than the 32mm (1¼in) diameter of the finished leg. This is best achieved by preparing a measuring gauge in thick card, set to a gap of about 35mm (1⅜in) which will just fit over the cylinder of wood when sufficient waste has been removed. Then measure and mark off the full length of the leg, the additional 19mm (¾in) at the top of the leg for the pin that will fit into the hole drilled to receive it in the underside of the seat, and the three 'bobbins' that decorate the leg, each one set at an interval that suits your taste.

Fashion the 'bobbins' with the parting tool and a narrow gouge, taper off the bottom of the leg, and reduce the portion at the top of the leg, for the pin, to a diameter of 19mm (¾in).

If you stop the lathe turning and examine the leg, you will note that its surface is still rather rough, and although it is true that by further careful use of the

Shape the main features of the leg, such as the 'bobbins', using the parting tool and a narrow gouge.

spindle gouge this can be refined to a comparatively smooth finish, there is always the danger of cutting down the diameter to the point where it is less than you want, in the certain knowledge that it will still need to be sandpapered.

The preferred method is to stop using the wood-turning tools with the diameter of the leg at 35mm (1⅜in), and take off the remaining 3mm (⅛in) by sandpapering. The paper recommended is a heavy-weight sheet, of medium grit, used in floor-sanding machines, which may be purchased from tool-hire depots that deal in such items. The sheets are quite expensive, but they last much longer than conventional sandpaper. Cut a small square of the abrasive paper, set the lathe turning again and work the paper continuously back and forth along the length of the leg, never allowing it to remain in one place for long. Keep checking the diameter using another card gauge cut to a gap of 32mm (1¼in).

Retrim the 'bobbins' with the parting tool and the narrow gouge, and finally rub down with fine-grade ordinary sandpaper, still with the lathe running. When the leg appears to be satisfactory and entirely smooth, remove it from the lathe and proceed to turn the second leg, and then the third and the fourth. Only when they have all been turned to the same pattern as the first leg, and compared with it to make certain that they are all identical, should the ends be trimmed, cutting away the unwanted waste with the tenon saw. Remember to allow 19mm (¾in) for the peg at the top of the leg.

The six backrest spindles and the three leg rails are turned in precisely the same way except that they are smaller in diameter and therefore do not need to be made from mopstick, but may instead be turned from softwood measuring 32 × 32mm (1¼ × 1¼in), in which instance you will firstly have to take off the four corners to produce the cylinder.

Each of the six backrest spindles is prepared to an overall length of 255mm (10in), and its maximum diameter, at the centre where there is a 'double bobbin' arrangement, is 19mm (¾in), tapering down at both ends to a diameter of 13mm (½in).

The three leg rails are divided into the

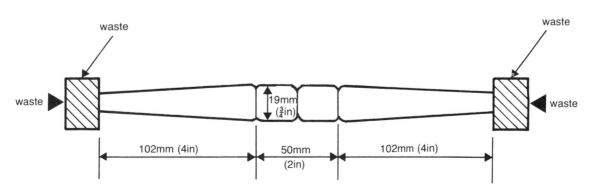

waste

waste

waste

19mm
(¾in)

102mm (4in)

50mm
(2in)

102mm (4in)

waste

waste

Main dimensions of the backrest spindle.

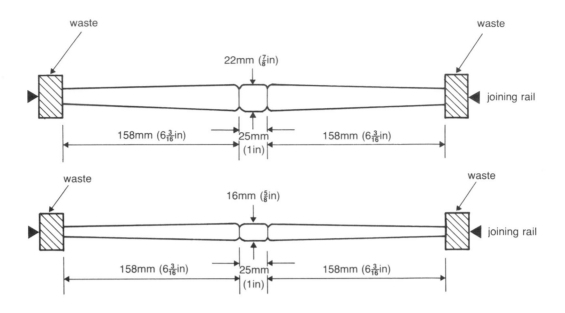

Main dimensions of the outer leg rails.

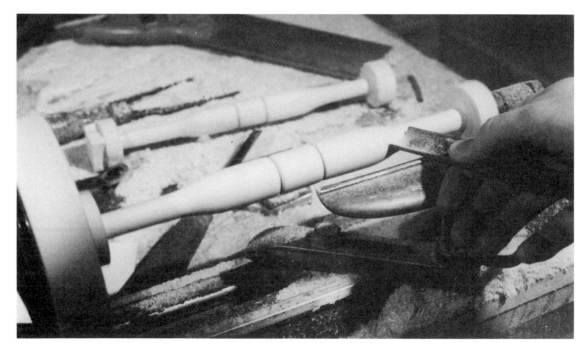

A leg rail receives its final tapering with the spindle gouge before being sandpapered to a smooth finish.

two outer rails which are both the same, each measuring 340mm (13⅜in) in length, with a maximum diameter at the centre of 22mm (⅞in) tapering to a diameter at each end of 16mm (⅝in); and the single joining leg rail, set between the two outer rails, which is also 340mm (13⅜in) long but only 16mm (⅝in) at the centre, tapering to 13mm (½in) at the ends. All of the 'bobbins', including those on the legs, measure 25mm (1in) long, the 'double-bobbins' measuring 50mm (2in).

Now that all of the chair components have been made, we are ready to consider the method of assembly. Here, yet again, very small variations in the mounting of the legs, or the positioning of the back-rest spindles in relation to the seat and the backrest, have a significant bearing on the appearance of the finished pro-

duct, and unless you have a jig which can guarantee drilling holes in precisely the same place and at the same angle every time, it is impossible to predict the exact outcome – which can have significant implications if you intend making a set of matching chairs.

The four holes drilled in the underside of the seat, to receive the pegs at the ends of the legs, are marked in such a way that their centres map out the four corners of a rectangle on the wood, a distance of 260mm (10¼in) separating the two front legs and the two back legs, and a distance of 235mm (9¼in) separating each front leg from its corresponding back leg. Having marked in their positions, drill each hole with a 19mm (¾in) diameter centre bit mounted in the handbrace, angling the drill in such a way that it

Drill the four holes for the legs in the underside of the seat with the handbrace, angled outwards.

splays outwards in the same direction as that intended for the leg. Bore to a depth of approximately 22mm ($\frac{7}{8}$in), taking care that the tip of the drill bit does not pass through to the topside of the seat.

An arrangement of six 13mm ($\frac{1}{2}$in) diameter holes is drilled at the rear of the seat's upper surface and the bottom edge of the backrest to receive the six backrest spindles, and the positioning and angling of these holes determine the manner in which the backrest meets the seat – whether it is set upright, or raked rearwards. Another factor is that the curve of the seat is greater than the backrest, causing a splayed effect, and you can choose either to set the distance between the holes equally for the seat and the backrest, or measure them slightly differently, so that the gaps are less for the seat than for the backrest, thus creating a divergence.

Drill all the holes to a depth of 13mm ($\frac{1}{2}$in), and make a test fitting of the six spindles. One tip is to take a piece of scrap wood and drill a 13mm ($\frac{1}{2}$in) diameter hole into it with the same centre bit, so that the tapered ends of the spindles can firstly be fitted. This will probably entail a certain amount of trimming with the chisel and twisting back and forth.

Next, measure and mark the hole positions in the four legs, setting each of these 130mm (5$\frac{1}{8}$in) up from the bottom end of the leg or halfway between 'bobbin' positions, whichever seems the more appropriate, and drill at an angle with a 16mm ($\frac{5}{8}$in) diameter centre bit to a depth of 19mm ($\frac{3}{4}$in). Finally, mark a position at the centre of the two main leg rails to receive the joining rail, and carefully bore out a hole of 13mm ($\frac{1}{2}$in) diameter to a depth of 9mm ($\frac{3}{8}$in).

A block of scrap wood has three holes of differing diameter bored in it, to provide a means of test-fitting the ends of the legs, backrest spindles and leg rails before proceeding with the assembling of the chair.

Make a test fitting of all the components, and when you are satisfied that they each join properly together, mix a quantity of wood glue and begin by assembling the backrest spindles to the seat and the backrest, tapping the assembly fully home with the mallet and a length of clean scrap wood. Last of all, apply glue to the four holes in the underside of the seat, to the peg projections at the top of the legs and to the rail holes, and attach the legs and their three rails.

When the glue has dried thoroughly, rub down the entire chair with fine-grade sandpaper and apply the desired finish.

The backrest spindles are glued into their receiver holes drilled in the seat.

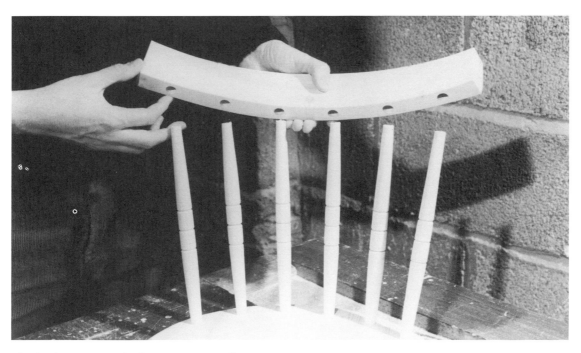

The backrest is attached to the six spindles.

The leg rails are assembled to the legs, and
these, in turn, joined to the seat.

CHAPTER EIGHT

CORNER CABINET

The hanging corner cabinet has an appeal and a usefulness of its own, and provides a neat and attractive display cupboard for the kitchen or the dining-room. Although the same style of cabinet is often made from one of the traditional hardwoods, such as oak or mahogany, its appearance in pine or any other knotty softwood should only serve to remind that there was a period when cupboards and cabinets were constructed from cheaper types of wood and painted, thus concealing the apparent shortcomings of the wood. In recent times, of course, it has become fashionable to strip off all the old paint and restore to the natural finish!

The first stage is to make the boards from which the top and bottom panels, the side panels and the interior shelves will be cut to size. The quickest and simplest method is to purchase several lengths of tongued-and-grooved softwood, measuring approximately 140 × 19mm (5½ × ¾in) excluding the tongue. Then glue these into boards of the required width, noting that three separate lengths of material will be needed to make up boards wide enough for the top, bottom and side panels, whereas only two lengths are needed for the shelves, as these are much narrower.

You can either make up small boards,

Cutting List

Top panel: one of 560 × 336 × 19mm (22 × 13¼ × ¾in)
Bottom panel: one of 560 × 336 × 19mm (22 × 13¼ × ¾in)
Door post: two of 788 × 76 × 19mm (31 × 3 × ¾in)
Rear post: one of 788 × 45 × 45mm (31 × 1¾ × 1¾in)
Top rail: one of 416 × 58 × 19mm (16⅜ × 2¼ × ¾in)
Side panel: two of 762 × 320 × 19mm (30 × 12⅝ × ¾in)
Door stile: two of 706 × 45 × 19mm (27¾ × 1¾ × ¾in)
Door rail: two of 356 × 45 × 19mm (14 × 1¾ × ¾in)
Long glazing bar: two of 344 × 19 × 13mm (13½ × ¾ × ½in)
Short glazing bar: eight of 156 × 19 × 13mm (6⅛ × ¾ × ½in)
Shelf batten: 306 × 25 × 13mm (12 × 1 × ½in)
Shelf: two of 460 × 242 × 19mm (18⅛ × 9½ × ¾in)

---

each short enough to cut out one of the panels at a time, individually, or one long board upon which all of the panels may be marked out and cut to size. Whichever method you prefer, begin by sawing the tongued-and-grooved wood to length, mix some wood glue, apply it

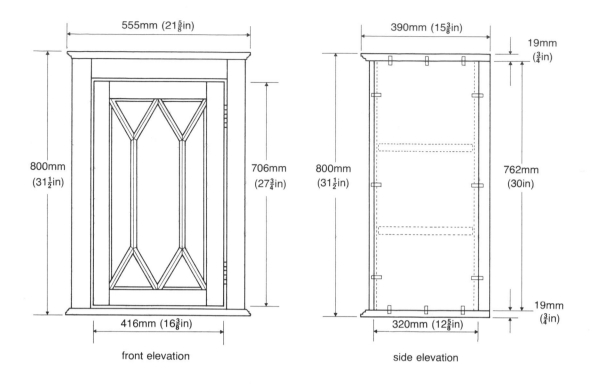

front elevation

side elevation

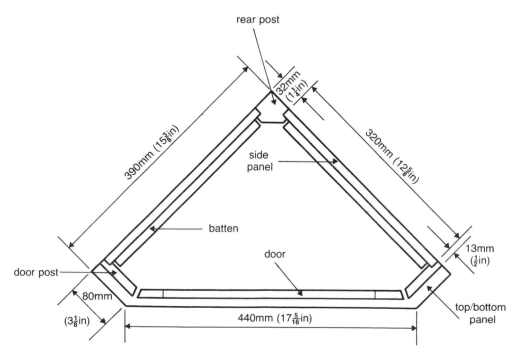

Main dimensions of the corner cabinet.

Cut out the top and bottom panels from the board with the jig-saw, cutting on the waste side of the marked lines.

carefully by brush to the tongues and the grooves, and slot the pieces together. Cramp them up tightly while maintaining the boards perfectly flat as the glue dries and hardens. Wipe away any surplus glue that squeezes out from the joins with a damp cloth.

After removing the cramps, plane down the tongues and grooves to produce flat edges in readiness for the marking out of the panels. Firstly, map out the shape of the two identical triangular top and bottom panels. In actual fact, these are not strictly triangular but could more accurately be called five-edged, as can be seen from the plan diagram, owing to the two short returns which accommodate the door posts. Measure and mark the panels using the tape measure, set square, a long straight edge and a pencil, and cut them to size using an electric

Place the cut-out top and bottom panels in contact with each other, in perfect alignment, hold them securely together in the vice, and plane down their edges.

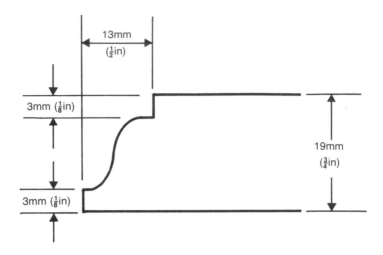

13mm
($\frac{1}{2}$in)

3mm ($\frac{1}{8}$in)

3mm ($\frac{1}{8}$in)

19mm
($\frac{3}{4}$in)

Dimensions of the Roman ogee moulding.

jig-saw fitted with a fine-toothed blade – an ordinary handsaw could be employed for this purpose, but will not produce such a smooth cut as the jig-saw – and then lightly plane all the edges.

The long front edge and the two short return edges of both panels should be given a moulded profile, such as that of a Roman ogee, or similar, using the electric router fitted with the appropriate cutter. You will need to have some experience of handling the router around corners in order to work the moulding successfully, and the best advice is to practise on a piece of identical scrap wood clamped to the workbench, before working on either of the two panels.

When you have successfully prepared the ogee profile in the three edges of each panel, rub them down with fine-grade sandpaper to remove loose strands of wood and to smooth out any slight irregularities caused by the passage of the router – not that there should be any!

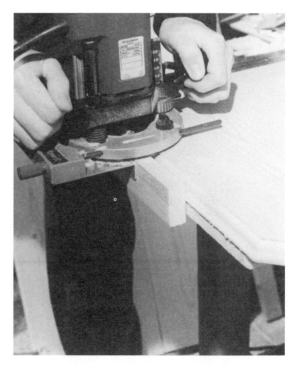

Prepare a Roman ogee edge-moulding on the three front edges of the top and bottom panel.

Next, take a length of material measuring 76 × 19mm (3 × ¾in) in cross-section and cut the two front posts, and another piece measuring 45 × 45mm (1¾ × 1¾in) for the rear post, also cut to the same length, allowing a little extra in each case for the tenon that will be prepared at both ends.

The two door posts and the rear post must be rebated to receive the side panels, and the width of these rebates should equal the 19mm (¾in) thickness of each side panel. In depth, they will be approximately 6mm (¼in) for the door posts and 13mm (½in) for the rear post. Set the marking gauge to each of the

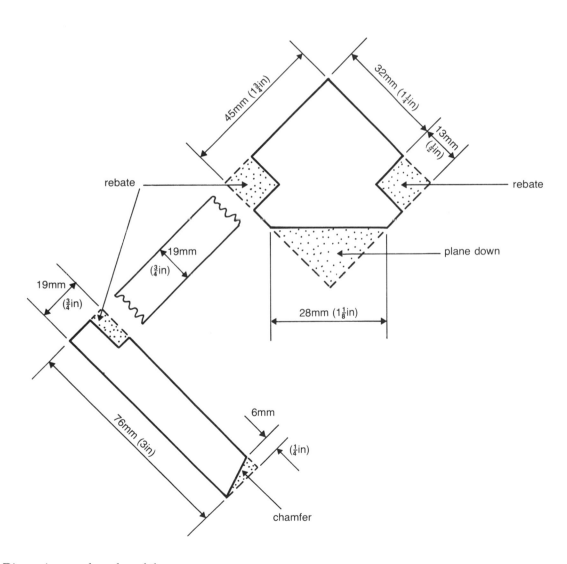

Dimensions and angles of the corners.

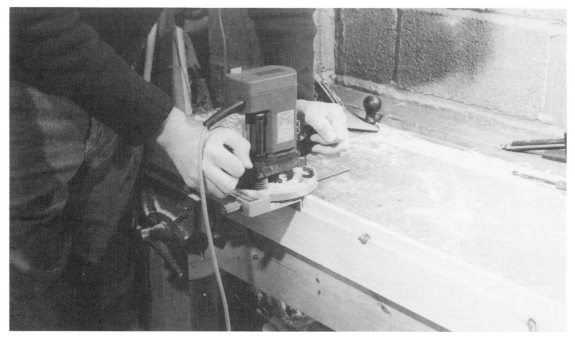

Preparing a rebate in one of the door posts with the router.

above dimensions and scribe the lines respectively on the three posts, preparing the rebates with the router or the plough plane.

Chamfer the two inside edges of the door posts with the smoothing plane in order to reduce the angle at which they meet the door. Indeed, even if it is your intention not to fit a cabinet door but to leave the front entirely open, it would still be desirable to carry out the chamfering. The correct amount to be chamfered can easily be determined by setting the marking gauge to 6mm ($\frac{1}{4}$in) and scribing a line along the inside face adjacent to the door position, leaving the outer face clear. Simply manipulate the plane at an angle to remove the required amount of waste while holding the piece securely in the workbench vice.

Also chamfer the front corner of the rear post to produce a flattened edge measuring 28mm (1$\frac{1}{8}$in) wide.

All three posts are attached to the top and bottom panels with mortise and tenon joints, the mortises being cut in the panels, with the tenons at both ends of each post. Mark in the mortises for the two door posts using the mortise gauge, setting the spurs to a gap of 9mm ($\frac{3}{8}$in), with the fence adjusted to scribe the lines parallel to the two short returns and inset by a distance of 16mm ($\frac{5}{8}$in) from the moulding. Set in the mortise at least 19mm ($\frac{3}{4}$in) from the outer edge of the panel, and measured to such a length that it comes to within 6mm ($\frac{1}{4}$in) of the chamfered edge of each door post.

The mortise at the rear, or apex, of each panel is best measured and marked in with a ruler and pencil, the guiding principle being that it should be large

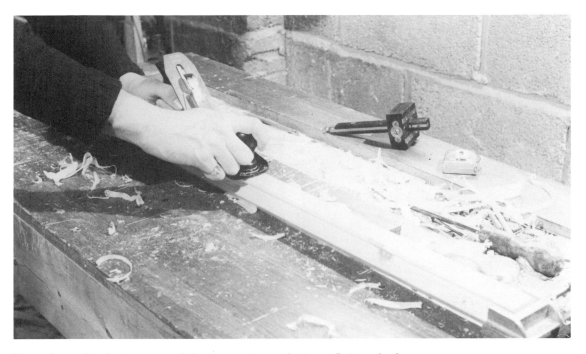

Plane down the front corner of the rear post, producing a flattened edge.

Carefully chop out the mortise for the rear post at the apex of the top and bottom panels.

enough to secure the matching tenon that will be cut in the rear post, but not so large as to weaken the apex and thus cause the right-angled corner of the panel to break off.

Remove most of the waste from each mortise with a 9mm (⅜in) diameter auger bit or centre bit mounted in the hand-brace, drilling just short of the depth where the point of the drill bit would begin to emerge through the opposite side of the panel. When a series of holes has been drilled within the marked-out area, carefully chop away the remaining waste with a 6mm (¼in) chisel and mallet, cutting to a depth of 13mm (½in).

Mark in corresponding tenons at the ends of the three posts, and cut off the waste with the tenon saw, cleaning up the four shoulders of each tenon with the 6mm (¼in) chisel. Gently tap all the joints

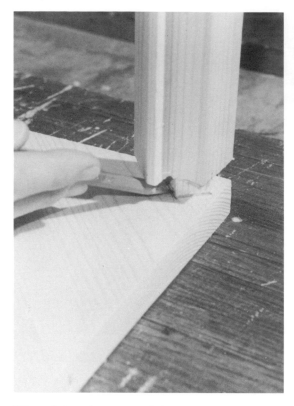

When fitting the tenon of the rear post into the mortise in the top or bottom panel, if the tenon is too large for the mortise, align the two pieces and mark a pencil line around the tenon to indicate by how much the mortise should be enlarged.

Cut the side panels to size and check that they fit into the rebates.

together to check that they fit fully home, taking care not to force them in too hard and risk splitting the panels as a consequence. If resistance is felt, trim the offending tenon or slightly enlarge the mortise by paring off tiny portions of wood with the chisel.

When all the joints fit neatly together, assemble the three posts to the top and bottom panels – without applying glue just yet – and measure and cut the two side panels so that they fit exactly into the housing rebates and lie flush with the top and bottom panels.

Cut a length of 58 × 19mm ($2\frac{1}{4}$ × $\frac{3}{4}$in) material to fit between the two door posts where it forms the top rail, trimming the two ends to match the chamfers of the posts. When fitted in position, it should butt up against the two posts and the underside of the top panel.

The two side panels and the top rail are next secured in their respective positions with dowel joints. Each side panel will need three dowel joints on all of its four edges, the dowels being spaced at regular intervals. The top rail is dowel-jointed in two places to the top panel, with a single dowel joint between the end-grain and the chamfered edges of the door posts. Mark in the positions of all the dowel holes, making sure that they all correspond perfectly between adjoining surfaces. Where the dowel holes occur in the edges or ends of the sides and the top rail, their positions should be set precisely halfway across the 19mm ($\frac{3}{4}$in) thickness of the material by adjusting the fence of the marking gauge until the pointer makes its mark centrally on the edge, and scribe a line along the full length of the edges and end-grains, measuring and marking off the positions as required, in pencil.

Drill out the dowel holes with a 6mm ($\frac{1}{4}$in) diameter auger bit mounted in the handbrace, taking great care when boring the holes in the top and bottom panels, and the door post rebates, to prevent the drill bit from breaking through. This is especially a danger with the rebates in the door posts, where the thickness of the wood is scarcely 13mm ($\frac{1}{2}$in).

Once all the dowel holes have been drilled, measure the combined depths for each joint, which should add up to at least 25mm (1in) – the holes in the edges and end-grains of the side panels and top rail being virtually unrestricted – and cut all the dowels to this length from 6mm ($\frac{1}{4}$in) diameter material, bevelling the ends in a pencil sharpener, and cutting a shallow glue channel along their length with a saw-blade.

Mix a quantity of wood glue and assemble the joints. Begin by joining the two side panels to the rear post, then add

Assemble the side panels to the two door posts and the rear post.

the door posts and the top rail. When this sub-assembly is complete, joint it to the bottom panel, and finally, add the top. In tapping all the joints fully home, apply the necessary pressure with the mallet through a large clean block of scrap wood to spread the impact and reduce the chance of splitting any of the panels, particularly towards the rear corner of the top and bottom panels. Cramp up the assembly and allow time for the glue to dry and set hard.

Decorate the inside corners between the two sides and the top and bottom panels with lengths of narrow quadrant material, cutting it to fit neatly between the door posts and the rear post. Glue these in place, locating each strip securely to its corner with pins while the glue dries.

The next step is to prepare and fit the four shelf battens. These are measured and cut from 25 × 13mm (1 × ½in) softwood, and, as with the quadrant strips for the top and bottom corners, the battens fill the gap between the door posts and the rear post. Two No. 8 screw-holes are drilled in each batten for the screws that fix them to the side panels, the holes being marked in by 63mm (2½in) from either end; and a single No. 10 screw-hole is drilled in the centre of the batten, to attach the finished cabinet to the wall, thus providing four fixture positions.

You can decide for yourself the height at which the battens should be mounted inside the cabinet, depending on how much space you want to have between the individual shelves; but, as a rule, it pays to spread them evenly apart, splitting the height of the cabinet into equal thirds. Make sure that you arrange each pair of battens at the same level before marking in the screw holes with a

Fit the shelf battens to the inside surface of the two side panels with glue and screws.

bradawl and enlarging them by driving in a No. 8 screw. It is not possible to drill the holes in the usual way, because there would not be room inside the cabinet to accommodate the handbrace, although you may just be able to use a hand-drill. Glue and screw the battens in place with 25mm (1in) No. 8 countersunk woodscrews.

Mark out the shelves on the 19mm (¾in) thick boards made up from the tongued-and-grooved material. It is best to prepare a cardboard template first. Actually, a half-template is easier to mark and cut out, following an imaginary centre line that splits the bottom panel into two symmetrical halves. Set the template 3mm ($\frac{1}{8}$in) back from the inside front edge of the two door posts, and then transfer the pattern on to the boards, cut out with the jig-saw or handsaw, trim the edges carefully with the smoothing plane and rest the shelves on their battens.

A nice finishing touch for the outside of the cabinet is to fit a length of shaped beading to the lowest part of the top rail. This may either be salvaged from old furniture, purchased as a ready-made strip from a local DIY shop or, of course, you can prepare your own if you are equipped with an appropriate cutter for the router or the plough plane. Cut a single long length to fit along the top rail, and two short lengths to run in a continuation across the door posts. Trim the ends of the beading so that they butt tightly up against one another, allowing for the angle between the top rail and the door posts, and fix to the cabinet with wood glue and veneer pins.

At this point, you have a choice. You can either leave the cabinet open, in which case it only remains to apply the desired finish to the wood, or you can make a glazed door to enclose the interior.

THE OPTIONAL DOOR

The door consists of a standard frame, made up from rebated rails and stiles, to which glazing bars may be added for a more attractive appearance. The pattern of these glazing bars can be as simple and straightforward or as complex and fancy as your imagination and woodworking talents will permit. It is not the easiest of

tasks, and you will have to make and shape every component yourself. That's why you have the option of leaving the cabinet open!

The main frame of the door is easy enough to construct and follows the normal routine of having two stiles and two rails, all joined together with mortise and tenon joints. A corner-round moulding, with a small lip, is worked along the front-facing inside edge of each piece, with a rebate cut behind it to receive the glass.

The rails and stiles are all made from 45×19mm ($1\frac{3}{4} \times \frac{3}{4}$in) material. It is probably best to work the edge-moulding and the rebate on a single long piece of wood before measuring and cutting it up into the four individual sizes, as this will permit the cutting and rebating to be carried out in a continuous run, ensuring greater accuracy.

Set the marking gauge to scribe a line exactly halfway across the 19mm ($\frac{3}{4}$in) thickness of the material, and mark the line along what will be the inside edge. Clamp the wood to the top of the workbench, or in the vice, with the marked edge uppermost, and cut a rebate on one side of the line to a depth of 3mm ($\frac{1}{8}$in) using the router or the plough plane fitted with a straight cutter. Having completed the rebate satisfactorily, change the cutter to one which produces a corner-round profile and, leaving a lip of about 2mm ($\frac{3}{32}$in) width, work a curved edge along the opposite corner to that of the rebate.

An identical profile is cut for the glazing bars but, as these are much smaller in cross-section than the stiles or rails and, therefore, impossible to clamp individually in the vice, an alternative method must be employed. The finished

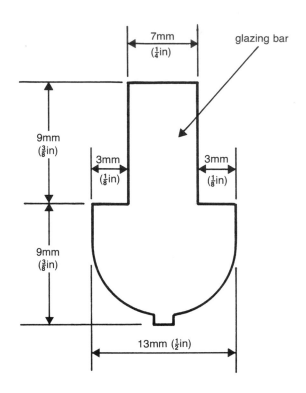

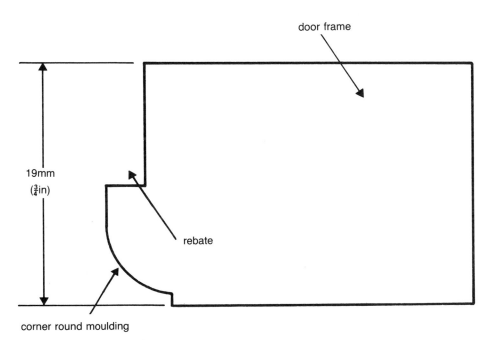

Cross-sectional view of the door frame.

glazing bars measure 13mm ($\frac{1}{2}$in) wide, so take a piece of softwood material measuring 13mm ($\frac{1}{2}$in) thick and at least 95 mm (3$\frac{3}{4}$in) wide and long enough to provide sufficient length for the vertical glazing bars, allowing a generous surplus at each end. A piece of tongued-and-grooved material would be suitable for this task, once the tongue or the groove has been planed down to a square and level edge.

Set the mortise gauge so that there is a gap of 9.5mm ($\frac{3}{8}$in) between the two spurs and a further 9.5mm ($\frac{3}{8}$in) gap between the fence of the gauge and the nearer of the spurs. Working the fence against the long straight planed edge, scribe a pair of parallel lines on both sides of the material, the area between these lines denoting the width to be rebated.

Clamp the piece of material in the vice, planed edge uppermost, and work a curved profile on both corners, using the router with the corner round cutter fitted, leaving a raised lip along the centre of the edge, measuring approximately 2mm ($\frac{3}{32}$in) wide. To achieve this particular cut, work the router firstly along one side of the wood, and then back again along the opposite side.

Now place the wood flat on the workbench and cut a rebate between the two scribed lines, using the router or plough plane fitted with the straight cutter, and rebating to a depth of 3mm ($\frac{1}{8}$in) on each side. When the glazing bar has been shaped to the required pattern, cut it away from the rest of the board with a sharp knife, then plane the board smooth and flat, and repeat the same procedure until you have sufficient numbers of glazing bars.

Having completed all the component parts for the door, the next stage is to cut the mortises and tenons for the joints between the stiles and the rails. Measure the two stiles to length but allow extra amounts at the ends so that the mortises can be cut safely without risking splitting

The edge-moulding is mitred and the adjacent surface of the wood trimmed flat for the marking of the mortise or the tenon.

the wood. Note that the edge moulding – that portion that is raised beyond the rebate on each of the stiles and rails – is effectively mitred at all four corners, so that the sections on the stiles where the mortises are marked in and cut must firstly be levelled flush with the rebate. They will thus form a flat edge, with the edge moulding trimmed at an angle of 45 degrees in readiness to receive a similarly prepared edge moulding on the rail. Actually, it is best to allow a little too much edge moulding at this point, which can be trimmed back further when the mortise and tenon joints are cut and ready to be fitted together.

Set the gap between the spurs of the mortise gauge to 6mm (¼in), and adjust the fence so that they scribe a pair of parallel lines centrally along the flat edge. Arrange for the mortise to be inset by 13mm (½in) from the end of the stile and 6mm (¼in) from the mitred edge moulding. The mortise should be stopped at a depth of 32mm (1¼in), and is prepared by firstly drilling several holes along the length of the marked out area using a 6mm (¼in) auger bit mounted in the handbrace, and then chopping out the remaining waste with the 6mm (¼in) chisel.

Mark a corresponding tenon at each end of both the rails using the mortise gauge set as for marking the mortises, remove the waste to create the first pair of shoulders, set in the tenon to match the setting in of the mortises, and cut off the unwanted wood, trimming with the chisel until the two parts of the joint fit fully together. The mitring of the edge moulding may require further trimming to achieve a perfect fit.

When all four mortise and tenon joints are complete, glue the door frame together, check that all the joints form exact right-angles, and cramp up the assembly while the glue dries and hardens. If you have taken the precaution of cutting the stiles too long, and leaving projections at either end, these may be sawn and planed flush with the outer edge of the rails once the glue has set fully.

Chamfer the outside edges of the door stiles to match the angles of the door-post edges.

The next stage is to cut and fit the glazing bars. Begin by drawing your chosen pattern on to a sheet of paper and cutting it into narrow strips to represent the joints between the bars. With careful

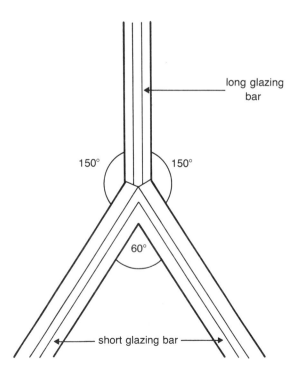

Construction of the glazing bars.

A simple paper template allows the glazing bars to be cut with their ends suitably angled to provide a strong three-way joint.

The fitting of the final glazing bar into position provides a rigid interlocking structure. Apply glue to all the abutting surfaces.

measurement and accurately drawn angles, mark out the glazing bars – arranging the paper template to give the correct angle for the special three-way joints where they meet – and cut them to shape.

The door frame needs to be notched at each point where the glazing bars join up with it, and the process of building up the segmented glass panels requires a lot of patience and a high degree of skill. Take a tip: never cut too much waste from the door frame or the glazing bars at a time, but trim each one gradually until they all slot together to form a single interlocked structure. When the final bar goes into position, the whole assembly should hold together of its own accord. Obviously, it needs to be made permanent with wood glue, so mix a small amount, apply it by brush to each joining surface and re-assemble the bars in their correct places.

Apply the desired finish to all the surfaces of the cabinet, the door and the two shelves. Fit brass hinges to the one edge of the door, and a small cabinet lock on the opposite edge, which will need a shallow recess to take the lock. A key-hole should be cut through the thickness of the stile and a small brass liner tapped into the outside face of the hole.

Your local glass supplier will cut 2mm ($\frac{3}{32}$in) clear glass to fit the glazed panels of the door and these should be puttied in.

Place the finished cabinet in the corner of the room, mark in the screw positions and prepare four holes in the wall using a masonry drill. Mount the cabinet, and fix it to the wall with four 50mm (2in) No. 10 countersunk woodscrews.

CHAPTER NINE

KITCHEN PREPARATION TROLLEY

The kitchen preparation trolley is a useful mobile work platform for the kitchen where you can prepare food as well as using it to store utensils. Our example is based on a standard wooden trolley with four legs, a bottom shelf and decorative castor wheels. The main difference is that the plain top shelf has been replaced by a work surface with drawer space beneath. A pull-out tray provides an additional feature.

Take four pieces of 32 × 32mm ($1\frac{1}{4}$ × $1\frac{1}{4}$in) material and cut the legs to length, allowing for the tenon at the top of each one which requires an additional 19mm ($\frac{3}{4}$in).

Cut two top end rails from 45 × 32mm ($1\frac{3}{4}$ × $1\frac{1}{4}$in) material, deliberately measuring overlength for the time being if you wish to give yourself a margin of safety when cutting out the mortises without the risk of splitting the ends. Mark in the positions of the mortises on the undersides to receive the leg tenons. For this, the mortise gauge is set to 13mm ($\frac{1}{2}$in) and the pointers arranged to mark the wood centrally. Each mortise is then set in by 3mm ($\frac{1}{8}$in) from its inside edge and 9mm ($\frac{3}{8}$in) from the outside.

Drill out the initial waste with a 13mm ($\frac{1}{2}$in) diameter centre bit, making certain

Cutting List

Leg: four of 834 × 32 × 32mm ($32\frac{13}{16}$ × $1\frac{1}{4}$ × $1\frac{1}{4}$in)

Top side rail: two of 483 × 45 × 32mm (19 × $1\frac{3}{4}$ × $1\frac{1}{4}$in)

Top end rail: two of 455 × 45 × 32mm ($17\frac{15}{16}$ × $1\frac{3}{4}$ × $1\frac{1}{4}$in)

End panel: two of 406 × 145 × 13mm (16 × $5\frac{11}{16}$ × $\frac{1}{2}$in)

Dividing panel: one of 442 × 162 × 13mm ($17\frac{3}{8}$ × $6\frac{3}{8}$ × $\frac{1}{2}$in)

Tray rail: two of 455 × 38 × 19mm ($17\frac{15}{16}$ × $1\frac{1}{2}$ × $\frac{3}{4}$in)

Bottom side rail: two of 455 × 45 × 19mm ($17\frac{15}{16}$ × $1\frac{3}{4}$ × $\frac{3}{4}$in)

Bottom end rail: two of 395 × 45 × 19mm ($15\frac{9}{16}$ × $1\frac{3}{4}$ × $\frac{3}{4}$in)

Drawer front: four of 222 × 142 × 19mm ($8\frac{3}{4}$ × $5\frac{9}{16}$ × $\frac{3}{4}$in)

Drawer side: four of 442 × 142 × 13mm ($17\frac{3}{8}$ × $5\frac{9}{16}$ × $\frac{1}{2}$in)

Drawer bottom panel: two of 430 × 205 × 6mm ($16\frac{15}{16}$ × $8\frac{1}{16}$ × $\frac{1}{4}$in)

Tray end: two of 380 × 45 × 19mm (15 × $1\frac{3}{4}$ × $\frac{3}{4}$in)

Tray side: two of 495 × 19 × 13mm ($18\frac{7}{8}$ × $\frac{3}{4}$ × $\frac{1}{2}$in)

Tray bottom panel: one of 492 × 363 × 6mm ($19\frac{3}{8}$ × $14\frac{1}{4}$ × $\frac{1}{4}$in)

Top shelf: one of 476 × 406 × 19mm ($18\frac{3}{4}$ × 16 × $\frac{3}{4}$in)

Bottom shelf: one of 476 × 406 × 19mm ($18\frac{3}{4}$ × 16 × $\frac{3}{4}$in)

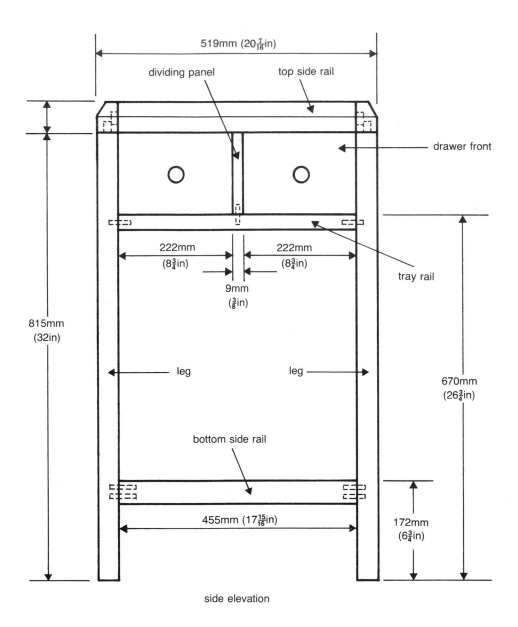

519mm (20$\frac{7}{16}$in)

dividing panel

top side rail

drawer front

222mm (8$\frac{3}{4}$in)

222mm (8$\frac{3}{4}$in)

9mm ($\frac{3}{8}$in)

tray rail

815mm (32in)

leg

leg

670mm (26$\frac{3}{4}$in)

bottom side rail

455mm (17$\frac{15}{16}$in)

172mm (6$\frac{3}{4}$in)

side elevation

Main dimensions of the kitchen preparation trolley.

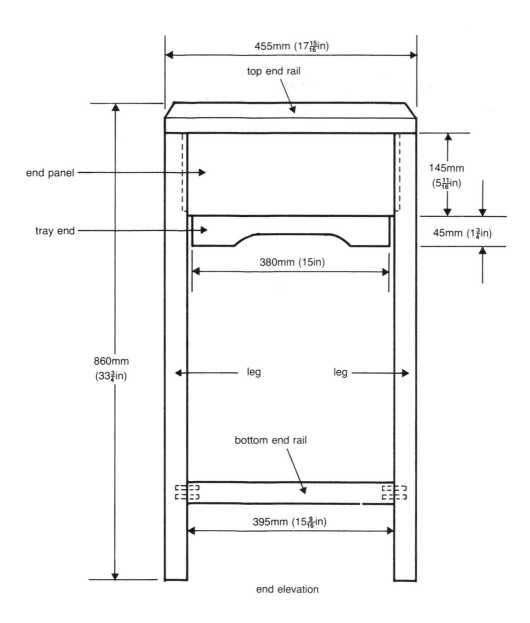

455mm (17$\frac{15}{16}$in)

top end rail

end panel

145mm
(5$\frac{11}{16}$in)

tray end

45mm (1$\frac{3}{4}$in)

380mm (15in)

860mm
(33$\frac{3}{4}$in)

leg   leg

bottom end rail

395mm (15$\frac{9}{16}$in)

end elevation

Main dimensions – end view.

that the pointed tip of the bit is placed very carefully inside the marked-out mortise position so that the circle described by the drill occurs precisely inside the scribed lines. Then finish chopping out each mortise with a chisel, cutting to a depth of just over 19mm (¾in). Actually, although it might seem obvious to use a 13mm (½in) chisel since this is exactly equal to the width of the mortise, you will find that the wood offers less resistance if you employ a 6mm (¼in) chisel, especially if you have marked and cut each top end rail to length. For the drilling and chiselling out, either hold the piece securely in the vice or clamp it firmly on top of the workbench using a small clamp which can be fastened at one end of the worktop.

Mark in the tenon at the top of each leg, using the same mortise gauge setting, squaring around the leg at the required 19mm (¾in) distance from the end, sawing off the waste with the tenon saw and measuring and marking in the second pair of shoulders to match the amount by which the mortise is set in at each end. Finally, trim the tenon with the chisel until all four joints fit perfectly without binding tightly or being too loose.

Cut the two top side rails from the same 45 × 32mm (1¾ × 1¼in) material, allowing an extra amount for the tenons that will be cut at each end.

The next step is to cut the grooves in all four top rails to house the top shelf. The shelf is prepared from tongued-and-grooved boards measuring 140 × 19mm (5½ × ¾in). Firstly, take a length of board material and set the gap between the pointers of the mortise gauge until they match its thickness. Adjust the fence of the gauge until it is fixed at a distance of 6mm (¼in) from the nearer pointer and

Prepare the groove in each of the top rails with the router.

use this setting to scribe two parallel lines along the inside surface of each top rail, working the gauge fence against the upper edge of all the rails.

Each groove is best prepared with the electric router, although the plough plane may be used instead if you prefer. The depth of the grooves should be about 6mm (¼in). It may not be convenient or possible for you to cut the grooves in one go using a 19mm (¾in) cutter in either the router or the plough plane, in which case a smaller cutter should be fitted, and the position varied so that the groove is formed from several narrow cuts. This latter method may be preferred, since the smaller cutter offers less resistance and makes the tool easier – and probably more accurate – to use.

The top side rails have the groove cut

along their entire length, but in the case of the end rails each groove is stopped 25mm (1in) from either end, a 13mm (½in) or 19mm (¾in) chisel being used to square them off cleanly. The question arises as to how the rails are best held in position while the router or plough plane is manipulated along the marked groove lines. The vice offers the most reliable grip, but clearly enough of the material must project above the jaws of the vice in order for the tool, and its fence, to make an unhindered pass. If each rail is clamped too high in the vice, its jaws may not have sufficient material to grip and it could move suddenly as pressure is exerted on the cutting tool.

The answer is to take a length of wood measuring 45mm (1¾in) wide and clamp this in the vice immediately beneath the rail so that it provides a foundation, and if there is still any slight tendency for the rail to move, it could be clamped to this second piece of material using G-clamps and small blocks of scrap wood. Such improvisation can make the difference between a good clean cut formed perfectly within the marked lines and an uncertain wobbling cut which strays occasionally beyond the lines.

Next, the outside face of each rail is chamfered to provide a slope rather than a square top edge. This is not absolutely necessary and could be omitted if you have a preference for the latter. Begin by marking in the amount to be taken off, using a marking gauge to score a faint line halfway down the outer face and halfway across the thickness of the material along the top edge.

Once again, clamp each piece firmly in the vice, this time facing the other way

Prepare the chamfered edge with the smoothing plane or the spokeshave.

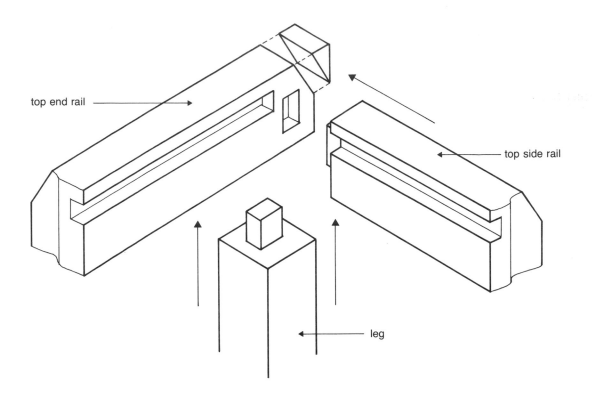

top end rail

top side rail

leg

Exploded view of the leg to top end rail joint.

up, and plane off the waste. The bevelled effect provides an attractive finish and is well worth the effort.

The two end rails are attached to the two side rails with mortise and tenon joints, the mortises being cut in the end rails and the tenons in the sides. A depth of 9mm (⅜in) for each joint is desirable; any more than that and there is a risk of cutting into the leg joints. If this seems rather shallow, bear in mind that the joints will be strengthened by the presence of the top shelf which is glued into its grooves.

The mortises are set to a width of 13mm (½in), positioned centrally with respect to the thickness of the joining side rail, and set in by 13mm (½in) top and bottom. Although the same method of preparation is used, starting with the drill and finishing with the chisel, each tool must be worked with great care to avoid cutting into the adjacent mortise.

Prepare matching tenons at the ends of the side rails, and trim the four joints so that the rails all fit neatly together to make a frame for the top shelf. Note that, at the moment, the end rails project beyond the chamfered side rails, but this will be attended to after the rails have been assembled to the top shelf.

The top shelf is composed of three tongued-and-grooved boards, each cut to length and slotted together. The overall

Marking in the mortise at one end of the end rail, using the mortise gauge.

The end rail is held firmly in a small benchtop clamp and the waste removed from the mortise, taking care not to split the wood.

Mark in the second pair of shoulders for the tenon and cut off the waste with the tenon saw.

length and width of the jointed boards can only be accurately determined by making a trial assembly of the four rails – without glue – and measuring the size of the top shelf, allowing for the depths of the four grooves. The two outer boards will require some planing down, and all three boards should be squared accurately to length before cutting to size. Fit the boards together and slot them into their grooves, tapping the tenons into their mortises. A certain amount of trimming may be necessary before a perfect fit is achieved, when the boards will lie snugly within their grooves and the side rails and end rails mate tightly up against each other.

Taking the assembly apart again, mix a small quantity of wood glue and apply it to the tongues and grooves of the top shelf boards, pressing them firmly home.

Brush more of the glue into the grooves of the side and end top rails, and to their mortise and tenon joints. Fit the three joined boards into the groove of one end rail, then slide the two side rails into position and finally tap down the second end rail using the mallet and a clean block of scrap wood.

Cramp up the assembly so that the joints are kept under firm pressure while the glue dries and hardens, wiping away any excess glue that usually squeezes out from the joints. After a day or so, remove the cramps and prepare to remove the small projections at the ends of the two end rails, thus making them flush with the chamfered outer surfaces of the side rails. The bulk of the waste may be re-moved by simply propping up the

Three tongued-and-grooved boards are joined together to make the top shelf.

assembly on the workbench and cutting off most of the projecting material with the tenon saw, taking care not to work the saw blade too closely to the adjoining side rails, whose surfaces could easily be marked by the teeth of the blade.

Next, clamp the assembly securely upright in the vice and plane off all the surplus wood. An electric planer is an ideal tool for this job because it can be set to the minimum thickness of cut and worked very slowly and carefully across the end-grain of each end rail, always directed inwards towards the side rail in order to avoid splitting the exposed edge of the end grain. Indeed, this is a good opportunity to plane very lightly over all of the rail surfaces, as there will inevitably be some scratches and marks caused by the cutting and putting together of the joints.

The two top end panels are now jointed to the legs using housing joints. Each panel is 13mm ($\frac{1}{2}$in) thick and mounted flush with the inside face of its two supporting legs. Set the pointers of the mortise gauge to a gap of 6mm ($\frac{1}{4}$in) and adjust the fence so that they mark the end panels centrally. Mark in the housing groove on all four legs, arranging for the length of each groove to be 13mm ($\frac{1}{2}$in) shorter than the width of the end panels. Cut out the grooves using the electric router or plough plane fitted with a 6mm ($\frac{1}{4}$in) cutter, set to a depth of 6mm ($\frac{1}{4}$in). In each case, stop the router at the point where the groove ends and square off neatly with a 6mm ($\frac{1}{4}$in) chisel cut.

Measure the two end panels accurately to length, allowing for the tongue that must be prepared at each end, cut to size

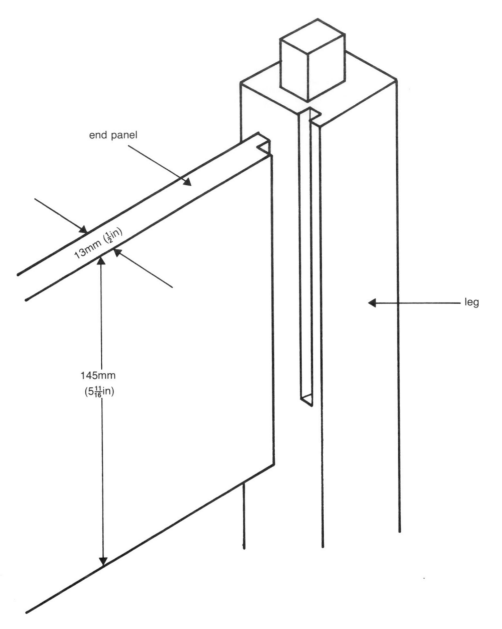

end panel

13mm ($\frac{1}{2}$in)

145mm
(5$\frac{11}{16}$in)

leg

Leg to end panel housing joint.

and then mark in each tongue, using the same mortise gauge setting, and remove the shoulders with the tenon saw. At the bottom edge, set in both tongues by 13mm ($\frac{1}{2}$in) to match the grooves, and check the joints for a good fit, trimming where necessary with the chisel. Make a

test fitting of the end panel and its two supporting legs to the underside of the top shelf assembly: if you have measured and cut the end panel joints with the required accuracy, the tenons of the legs should tap into the mortises of the end rails, the end panel be retained

Fit the end panel and its two supporting legs experimentally into the top shelf assembly.

fully in its grooves, and the two legs run parallel along their entire length.

Remedial action at this stage can only consist of reducing the length of the end panel if it is found to be slightly too long by trimming back the shoulders of the tongues. If the end panel is found to be loose-fitting between the legs, the only solution would be to discard it, take a piece of fresh material and make a new one.

Once both leg and end panel assemblies fit satisfactorily in position, place the top shelf assembly upside down on the workbench, with all four legs and two end panels temporarily fitted, and cut the dividing panel that separates the drawers from each other. Notch it at each end so that it fits tightly up against the underside of the shelf boards and cut to

Cut the dividing panel to size, and prepare a notch at each end to enable the panel to fit between the top side rails of the top shelf assembly.

exactly the same depth as the end panels. This may be checked quite easily by placing a straight-edge across the end panels – if the dividing panel is too wide, the straight-edge will rock, and if it is too narrow, you will see a gap. Obviously, it is preferable to start with a dividing panel that is somewhat too wide because it can be planed down by trial and error until it aligns perfectly.

Note that the two exposed end-grains of the dividing panel should not lie flush with the outer faces of the top side rails, but are located 4mm ($\frac{3}{16}$in) short. This leaves room to accommodate thin strips of prepared matching redwood which cover the end-grain, although it is prob-

ably best to leave their preparation until the two drawers have been constructed and fitted.

Mark in the positions of all four bottom shelf rails, together with the two dowel holes used to attach the end of each rail to the leg. Each rail is prepared from 45 × 19mm ($1\frac{3}{4} \times \frac{3}{4}$in) material and has a shelf groove cut along its inside face in the same way as the top shelf fits into the top rails, two parallel lines being scored to a width of 19mm ($\frac{3}{4}$in), and set down 6mm ($\frac{1}{4}$in) from the top edge, using the mortise gauge.

Cut the rails slightly overlength and prepare the grooves with the router or plough plane to a depth of 6mm ($\frac{1}{4}$in).

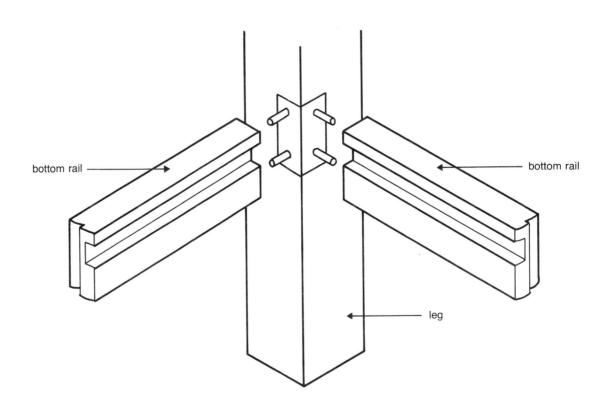

Leg to bottom rail dowel joint.

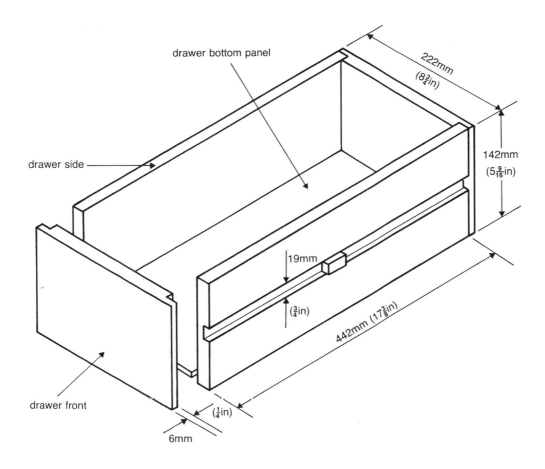

drawer bottom panel

222mm
(8¾in)

drawer side

142mm
(5 9/16 in)

19mm

(¾in)

442mm (17⅜in)

drawer front

(¼in)

6mm

Main dimensions of the drawer.

Finally, measure and mark each rail to its correct length, squaring all around and cutting with the tenon saw.

The dowel-hole positions are best marked on the end-grain of the bottom rails and the two adjacent surfaces of each leg using a card template to guarantee absolute accuracy. Cut out a piece of card identical in shape to the cross-section of the rail material – allowing for the inset groove – and mark in two tiny holes with a panel pin to represent the dowel positions. Transfer these pin-point markings on to the four rails and four legs, and bore out all the holes with a 6mm (¼in) diameter auger bit. You will find that the holes in the legs meet within the wood, and those bored into the end-grain of each bottom rail should be drilled to a depth of approximately 19mm (¾in).

Cut sixteen dowels from 6mm (¼in) dowelling material, each 25mm (1in) long, chamfering the ends by giving a couple of twists in a pencil sharpener and lightly sawing a glue channel along their

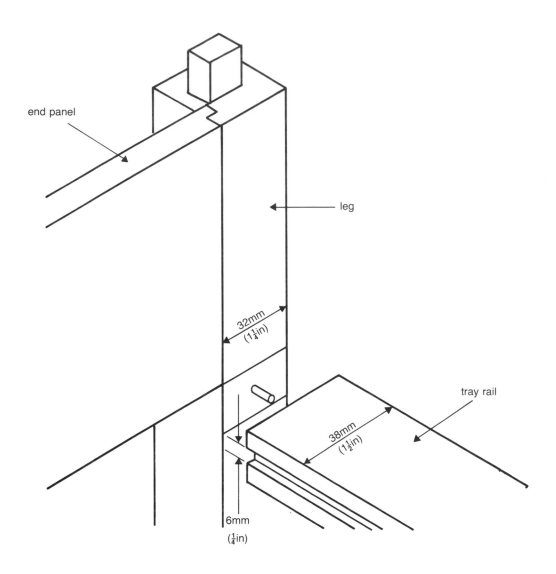

end panel

leg

32mm
$(1\frac{1}{4}in)$

38mm
$(1\frac{1}{2}in)$

tray rail

6mm
$(\frac{1}{4}in)$

Leg to tray rail dowel joint.

length. Glue the dowels into their receiver holes in all four legs, tapping them home with the mallet, but do not yet attempt to joint the bottom rails.

Prepare the two tray rails. These measure 38 × 19mm ($1\frac{1}{2}$ × $\frac{3}{4}$in) in cross-section, and can be obtained directly from tongued-and-grooved boards, since the groove is already worked along one edge, which can be marked and cut to the required width; the matching tongue is present on the opposite edge, and thus can be employed for the tray side. Cut the two tray rails to length and mark in

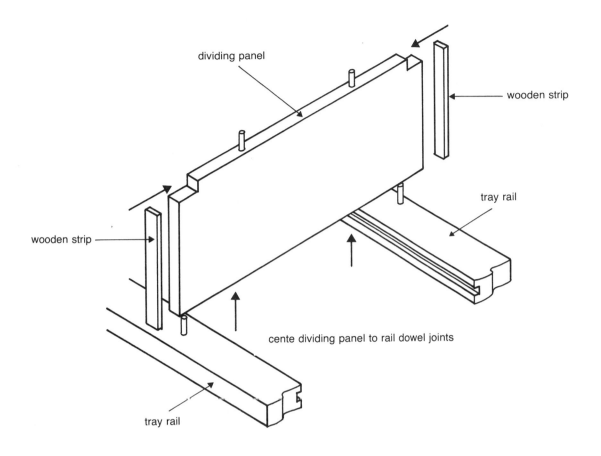

dividing panel

wooden strip

tray rail

wooden strip

cente dividing panel to rail dowel joints

tray rail

Dimensions of the centre dividing panel.

the position of the single dowel which joins each end-grain to a leg – again, a card template should be prepared for accuracy.

Once more, make a test fitting of all the joints so that the dividing panel can be placed in its correct position, dividing the trolley into two equal halves, and dowel holes marked on its two main edges: two dowels fixing the dividing panel to the underside of the top shelf and a single dowel joining each tray rail to the bottom edge of the panel.

Cut eight more dowels, checking that

they each fit into their holes, allowing the main components of the trolley to be assembled.

Measure and mark three more tongued-and-grooved boards to length for the bottom shelf, fitting them together and then measuring them to the required width so that they occupy fully the grooves in the bottom rails.

Mix a large quantity of wood glue, apply it by brush to all the joints, dowels and grooves, and assemble the structure. When all the joints are fully in place, tie strong string around the end of the legs, placing soft pads between the string and the wood to avoid creating pressure marks, and tighten the string with a tourniquet. Wipe away all traces of excess glue with a damp cloth, and keep the string and tourniquet in position for at least a day while the glue dries and sets hard.

After removing the string binding, set the trolley upside-down on the ground – standing it on a protective layer of newspapers – and prepare to mount the castor wheels to the bottom end of the legs. Each leg is square in cross-section, and its centre can be marked easily by pencilling in two straight diagonal lines. At the point where these lines intersect, drill a 9mm ($\frac{3}{8}$in) diameter hole 38mm ($1\frac{1}{2}$in) into the end-grain of each leg using a long auger bit to ensure a straight cut. The choice of castor wheel is up to you: there are many types and sizes available. For example, the illustrated 'dinner wagon' castor is a 75mm (3in) diameter gold-coloured spoked wheel fitted with a rubber tyre. Its housing socket is tapped into the drilled hole with the mallet until its serrated shoulder takes hold. Then fit each castor wheel into its socket.

The drawers are designed to be opened from both sides and there is a built in limiter to prevent them from being pulled right out. The limiter comes in the form of the two guide-blocks upon which each of the drawers runs. The sides of the drawers have grooves cut along their length into which each block fits, but the drawer fronts act as a stop to the grooves and, therefore, once assembled, it is impossible to remove the drawers.

Cut all the drawer fronts to size, noting that there should be a clearance of 2mm ($\frac{3}{32}$in) or so separating them from the

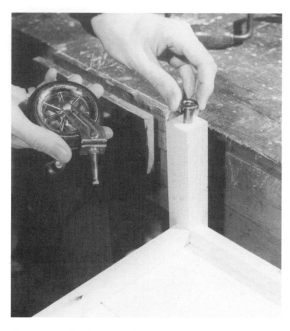

A castor wheel socket is fitted into a 9mm ($\frac{3}{8}$in) hole drilled at the bottom of the leg.

trolley frame. Next, cut the drawer sides, each of which should be the same width as the drawer front to which it will be attached, although not so thick.

Mark a groove along the outer face of each side piece, which for the time being should be cut well overlength, setting the groove exactly halfway down, 19mm ($\frac{3}{4}$in) wide. Prepare the grooves with the electric router or plough plane, cutting to a depth of 6mm ($\frac{1}{4}$in). Also run a groove along the lower inside face for each drawer's bottom panel, measuring 6mm ($\frac{1}{4}$in) wide, 4mm ($\frac{3}{16}$in) deep and set in 6mm ($\frac{1}{4}$in) from the bottom edge. A corresponding groove should be worked on the lower inside faces of all four drawer fronts, running the full length of each piece.

While the most suitable joint for a drawer construction is undoubtedly the

Cut a groove with the router midway across the width of a long board from which the four drawer sides will be marked out and sawn to length.

dovetail, in this instance such a joint would not be practicable because the provision of guide-blocks and grooved runners cut in the drawer sides means that each drawer must be partly assembled *in situ*. Dowel joints could be used, but the preferred method is to use lapped joints, where a simple rebate is worked at each end of the drawer front, into which the drawer side fits fully.

To mark the rebate, firstly square a line around the drawer front 13mm (½in) from each end, equal to the thickness of the drawer side. The depth of the rebate is 13mm (½in), so the marking gauge is set to this amount and a line scribed across the end-grain and both edges up to the squared line, the fence of the gauge bearing against the inner face of the drawer

front. Hold the piece firmly upright in the vice, and cut down with the tenon saw, working the blade on the waste side of the scribed lines, cutting as far as the squared line. Remove the drawer front from the vice, place it flat on a bench-hook and cut down on the waste side of the squared line to remove the unwanted wood. Clean up the rebate with the 6mm (¼in) chisel.

Measure the drawer sides to length: these should be equal to the overall width of the trolley, minus 13mm (½in) which is accounted for by adding together the two unrebated portions of the drawer fronts. Cut the drawer sides to size with the tenon saw and make a test fitting of each drawer.

Cut the bottom panel for the two drawers from 6mm (¼in) thick plywood, making allowance for the grooves into which it must fit.

For each drawer, glue the two sides to one drawer front, brush glue into the grooves and slide the bottom panel into place. Strengthen the lapped joints by tapping in 25mm (1in) panel pins, dovetail fashion, four in a row for each joint. When dry, slot this part-assembly into the trolley and mark the position of the two channels on the outside faces of the drawer sides, ensuring that there is adequate clearance to prevent the drawer from binding against its frame. Cut two blocks of hardwood per drawer to act as drawer guides, each block measuring approximately 19 × 9mm (¾ × ⅜in) in cross-section and 32mm (1¼in) in length, and glue these in place halfway along the length of the trolley end panels and dividing panel.

When dry, slide the half-completed drawer into position, and fit the second drawer front. Add green baize to the

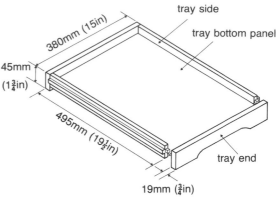

Dimensions of the tray.

Assembly of the drawer consists of applying glue to the joints between two drawer sides and one drawer front, each strengthened with panel pins, and adding the plywood drawer bottom. The second drawer front is not fitted until the partially-completed drawer has been mounted in position upon its guide blocks.

bottom, if desired. Fit drawer knobs or handles to suit your own personal choice.

Now that the drawers have been completed and fitted in place, the two exposed end-grains of the dividing panel can be attached. Their precise length, width and thickness will depend on your own efforts thus far. Trim the thin strips of redwood to size and glue them to the end-grain.

The tray is a simple structure consisting of two tray ends, cut from 45 × 19mm (1¾ × ¾in) material, two tray sides prepared from tongued material cut from the opposite end of the tongued-and-grooved board used to provide the tray rails, and a plywood bottom panel. The tray sides measure 19 × 13mm (¾ × ½in) in cross-section, not including the tongue, and these are jointed to the tray ends

with mortise and tenon joints. A rebate is cut along the inside face of the tray ends, 6mm (¼in), wide 6mm (¼in) deep, and set down by 19mm (¾in) from the top edge. A narrow portion is cut away from the bottom edge to form feet for the tray and to provide sufficient access in the middle for hands to grasp the tray.

The overall length of the tray ends should be just less than the distance between the tray rails, thus enabling the tray to be slid in and out from either end. The tray sides must be set so that the tongues project beyond the limits of the tray ends in order to fit into their housing grooves cut in the tray rails.

Measure and cut the plywood bottom panel to such a size that it fits into the grooves prepared in the tray ends and lies flush with the outside edges of the tray sides. The panel is glued in place, the small mortise and tenon joints tapped fully home and a series of 13mm (½in) veneer pins tacking the panel to the tray sides.

Rub down all the surfaces with fine-grade sandpaper before giving the trolley its finish.

CHAPTER TEN

SINGLE BED

A pine bed is a most attractive piece of furniture, providing a picture of warmth and solidity which is bound to enhance any bedroom. The main variations to consider are whether the bed should be built as a single or a double, a child's miniature, just large enough to take a cot mattress, or constructed in the form of two identical beds which may be inter-locked to form a double-decked bunk-bed arrangement. With so many options available, you must firstly decide for whom the bed is intended, and work out its overall dimensions from the size of the mattress. For instance, the illustrated bed is based on a standard single mat-tress measuring 1,880mm (74in) long and 915mm (36in) wide, giving a bed length of 1,980 (78in) and width of 990mm (39in).

The bed consists of several parts, of which the two chief constituents are the identical headboard and footboard; these are joined together by two long bed rails, and the rails support twelve slats upon which the mattress is placed. The reason why the two bed-ends are of the same size in this example is so that they are of equal height, and thus able to support an upper deck if required.

Each of the bed-ends is made up of two legs, a top and bottom rail, and a series of V-edged tongued-and-grooved boards slotted together to create panelling which

---

Cutting List

Leg: four of 864 × 45 × 45mm
       (34 × 1¾ × 1¾in)
Top rail: two of 978 × 120 × 19mm
       (38½ × 4¾ × ¾in)
Bottom rail: two of 978 × 95 × 19mm
       (38½ × 3¾ × ¾in)
Long rail: two of 1,967 × 95 × 19mm
       (77½ × 3¾ × ¾in)
Beam: two of 1,914 × 70 × 32mm
       (75⅜ × 2¾ × 1¼in)
Slat: twelve of 940 × 45 × 19mm
       (37 × 1¾ × ¾in)
Panelling: twenty-two of 432 × 89 × 13mm
       (17 × 3½ × ½in) V-edged tongued-and-grooved

---

fills the gap between the two rails. Both rails are fitted to the legs with mortise and tenon joints, and the panelling slots into grooves cut in the lower edge of the top rail, the upper edge of the bottom rail and the inside edge of the two legs. The two long bed rails which join the head-board to the footboard, creating a rigid structure, are each provided with a notched beam on their inside faces to strengthen them and provide a means of mounting the twelve slats.

A round knob is attached to the top of all four legs as decoration and serves one other purpose: if the bed is built as one of

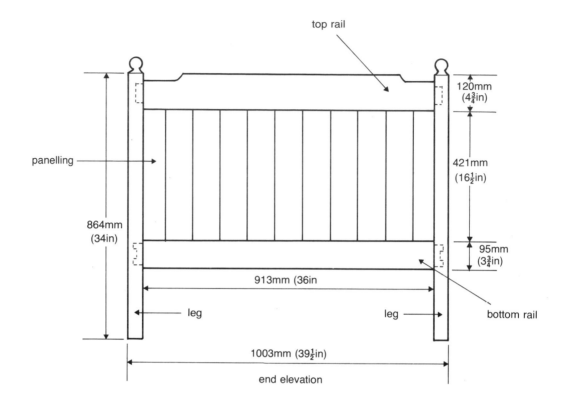

top rail

panelling

120mm
(4¾in)

421mm
(16½in)

95mm
(3¾in)

864mm
(34in)

913mm (36in

leg

leg

bottom rail

1003mm (39½in)

end elevation

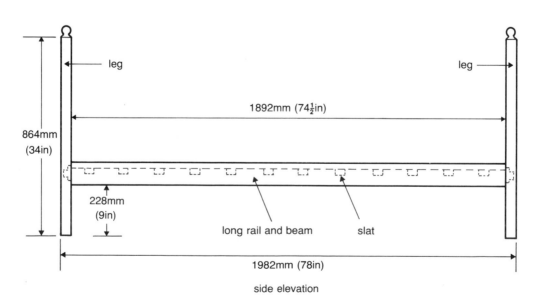

leg

leg

1892mm (74½in)

864mm
(34in)

228mm
(9in)

long rail and beam

slat

1982mm (78in)

side elevation

Main dimensions of the single bed.

a pair which fit together one on top of the other, each knob may be removed to reveal a hole into which a length of steel rod is inserted in order to join the legs of the top bunk to the legs of the bottom.

Start by measuring and cutting the four legs to the same length of 864mm (34in) each, ensuring that both ends are marked perfectly square and cut accurately with the tenon saw. Mark in the precise centre of each end-grain so that it can later be drilled with a hole to receive the ornamental knob or the steel-rod linkages for the double-decked arrangement, if desired, by pencilling two straight lines between diagonally opposite corners, the centre being the point where the lines cross one another.

Next, mark in the positions of the rails on each of the legs, comprising two markings on the inside face for the top rail and the bottom rail, and a single marking on an adjacent face for the long bed rail, set at the same level as the bottom rail. The lower edge of the bottom rail and long bed rail are placed 228mm (9in) up from the bottom of the leg, and the upper edge of the top rail is set 25mm (1in) down from the top of the leg, although it should be noted that this does not refer to the true upper edge, but to that part of the top rail which has been cut away at each end for decorative purposes. In actual fact, the true upper edge of the top rail lies more or less level with the squared end-grain of the leg before the knob is fitted.

Let us now consider the marking out and preparing of the mortises in each of the legs to receive the rail tenons. Here there must be a special arrangement that allows both of the lower rails to fit into their mortises, with the lower rail of the headboard and the footboard being per-

manently attached, but the long bed rail able to be fastened and dismantled so that the bed can be taken apart when necessary.

The most suitable way of arranging for this is to prepare both mortises in the usual way, so that they meet inside the wood, and then cut a double tenon for the headboard and footboard rails, in which there is a sizeable gap between two relatively narrow tenons, and a single-haunched tenon cut at each end of the long bed rails which fits into the gap. This arrangement is preferable to cutting mitres at the ends of the tenons because it permits the single tenon in the long rails to be housed as deeply as possible within the leg, giving greater strength to compensate for the fact that it is detachable, and only secured in place with a nut-and-bolt assembly. The top rail is fitted with a conventional mortise and tenon joint.

One other matter needs to be considered regarding these joints: each of the rails measures 19mm ($\frac{3}{4}$in) thick, compared with the 45mm ($1\frac{3}{4}$in) width of the four legs. If you follow the principle of making the width of the mortise equal to one-third the thickness of the wood in which it is to be cut, this suggests a precise width of 15mm ($\frac{19}{32}$in), although 16mm ($\frac{5}{8}$in) would be the closest realistic measurement. But this means that the waste cut from the sides of the tenons will measure only 1.5mm ($\frac{1}{16}$in) thick, which seems an absurdly small amount, so negligible as to be hardly worth while. Certainly it would be true to say that if the tenons were cut narrower, in order to give broader shoulders, the joint would be severely weakened. But if the mortises were cut to the same width as the rails so that the rails simply slotted in, inevitably the sides of the mortises would show and this would appear unsightly.

So the mortises will be 16mm (⅝in) wide. Take the mortise gauge and set the gap between the two spurs equal to the amount, using the width of a 16mm (⅝in) chisel as your guide. Adjust the fence of the gauge so that the spurs mark centrally across the 45mm (1¾in) width of the leg material, and then scribe a pair of parallel lines between each of the marked mortise positions. Now set these in slightly from the lines that denote the edges of the rails, using a square, pencil and tape measure; a setting in of 3mm (⅛in) will be quite sufficient.

All the mortises are cut to a depth of 32mm (1¼in) (with an additional 6mm (¼in) being cut out later from the central portion of the mortise that houses the long rail tenon, but this will be dealt with in due course). Begin by drilling a series of 16mm (⅝in) diameter holes along the marked-out area of each mortise using a 16mm (⅝in) diameter centre bit mounted in the handbrace, and boring to a depth of 32mm (1¼in). The depth of the holes can easily be gauged by applying a piece of sticky tape to the shaft of the drill bit.

When all of the holes have been drilled, chop out the remainder of the waste with the 16mm (⅝in) chisel and a mallet, working from the centre of the mortise outwards and finishing with a straight clean cut on the squared lines that denote the length of the mortise. Make sure that the sides of the mortise are perpendicular to the surface of the leg, and take greater care when chopping out the two adjacent mortises so that their ends coincide, and that the outer side of one is flush with the depth of the other, and vice versa.

The next step is to measure and mark out all of the tenons. In the case of the

Marking out a tenon with the mortise gauge.

tenons that are to be prepared at the ends of the headboard and footboard rails, these will need to be measured to a length of 32mm (1¼in) or slightly less, and the tenons for the long rails measured to a length of 38mm (1½in). Starting with the headboard and footboard rails, measure these to their full length, including the tenons, which should be 978mm (38½in) square right around at both ends, and cut to size with the tenon saw. Measure and mark off the length of each tenon, marking a squared pencil line around the sides and edges. Then adjust the fence of the mortise gauge so that the two spurs are set midway across the thickness of the material, scribing a pair of lines between the squared pencil markings and the end of the wood, as well as along the end-grain.

Each tenon has very narrow shoulders, so the waste may have to be removed with the aid of a broad-bladed chisel.

As you will observe, these gauged lines are set very close to the sides of the material, making it rather difficult to cut the tenons in the usual way. However, with great care and a steady hand, it is possible to cut away such a thin amount with the tenon saw, provided that the rail is securely clamped in the vice. The blade of the saw should, of course, work on the waste side of the line. Saw down as far as you can, then remove the rail from the vice, lay it flat on the workbench and score along the squared pencil line with a sharp knife and a straight edge for guidance. It should now be possible to pare off the thin slice of waste with a broad-blade chisel.

An alternative way of removing such a small amount of wood to form the shoulder of the tenon is to make several passes across the surface of the rail with the electric router fitted with the largest-diameter straight cutter you can find. The depth guide must be set carefully so that the cutter does not sink any deeper than the level of the scribed lines.

Do not be tempted to try tapping the blade of the chisel into the two lines marked on the end-grain, because wood will simply splinter off in the direction of the grain, and since the grain of this type of softwood has a habit of following a curved path, you may easily end up chopping away too much, resulting in an undersized tenon.

Set in the second pair of shoulders to match the setting in of the mortise, and make a test fitting of the joint. If you have marked and cut accurately, the tenon should fit into the mortise with gentle pressure and slide fully home. Often it binds in one or two places, in which case small slivers of wood should be pared from the mortise or the tenon until a proper fit is achieved.

Mark in the curved decorative lines at both ends of the top rail, and remove the waste with the jig-saw, trimming where necessary with the spokeshave. You may wish to add other flourishes of your own – a gentle curve running the full length of the rail, or a scalloped, shell-like edge which will have required a wider rail to begin with. Take a tip: it is probably best to opt for the most subdued form of patterning!

Now prepare the tenons for the long rails. It has already been mentioned that these should each measure 38mm (1½in) in length for reasons of strength and maximum rigidity. The length of each rail, including its tenons, should be 1,967mm (77½in). Remove the waste and

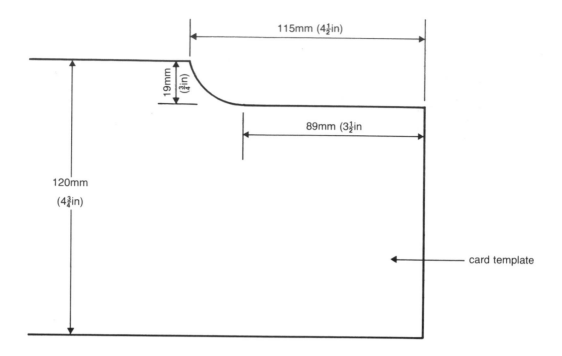

115mm (4½in)

19mm (¾in)

89mm (3½in)

120mm (4¾in)

card template

Dimensions of the template.

set in the second pair of shoulders, as previously, until the tenon fits most of the way into its mortise – the mortise still being 6mm (¼in) too short.

We have now reached the critical stage in the making of the tenons when those in the bottom rails of the headboard and footboard need to be split up into two narrow full-fitting tenons with a gap in the middle, into which the single-haunched tenons of the long rail can be fitted. Whereas the double tenons need not be particularly large, since they will in any case be glued and pegged in position, the long rail tenon must maintain as much of its size as possible, and therefore they are divided up as follows: the single tenon accounts for 50mm (2in) at the centre and the two outer tenons measure 19mm (¾in)

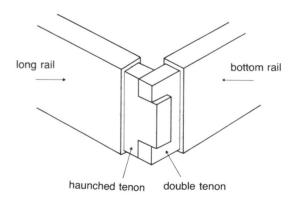

long rail

bottom rail

haunched tenon   double tenon

The interlocking tenon arrangement.

A bottom rail has a double tenon measured and marked on each of its main surfaces.

The waste portion between the two parts of the double tenon is removed by firstly making a series of saw-cuts within the marked-out area.

each. The haunches on either side of the single tenon and the middle portion of the double tenons project 15mm ($\frac{15}{32}$in) out from the tenon shoulders.

If you assemble the bottom rail loosely to both legs once the double tenons have been cut to size, you will be able to mark the bottom of the adjacent mortise in order to chop out a further 6mm ($\frac{1}{4}$in) so that the long rail tenon can fit fully in place. Take great care with this additional cutting out because you will be working deep inside the wood within a short distance of breaking through on the opposite side.

The space in between the top and bottom rail is now ready to be prepared to receive a panel made up from a series of boards cut from lengths of 89 × 13mm ($3\frac{1}{2}$ × $\frac{1}{2}$in) V-edged tongued-and-grooved

Remove the waste from the middle part of the double tenon by chopping away the sawn strips of wood with the chisel and mallet.

Mark in the groove that houses the boards used to fill the gap between the top and bottom rails by scribing two parallel lines between the mortises with the mortise gauge.

softwood. Eleven boards will be needed, each measuring 432mm (17in) long. They are fitted into a groove which is cut in the lower edge of the top rail, the upper edge of the bottom rail and the inside faces of the legs between the mortises. The groove measures 9mm ($\frac{3}{8}$in) in width and 13mm ($\frac{1}{2}$in) in depth and its position is marked on each piece of wood with the mortise gauge set to a gap of 13mm ($\frac{1}{2}$in), the fence of the gauge being adjusted so that the spurs mark the edges of the rails and the inside faces of the legs centrally.

The grooves may be cut either with the plough plane or the electric router fitted with a 9mm ($\frac{3}{8}$in) cutter, or indeed with a narrower cutter, taking more than one run. When each of the grooves has been prepared to your satisfaction, cut the eleven tongued-and-grooved boards to length and slot them together on a flat surface to create a single panel.

The groove between the mortises is prepared with the router.

Fit the rails back into the legs and measure *exactly* the distance between the two legs and the two rails. Transfer these measurements on to the panel to determine the positions at the ends of the boards, and at each end of the panel assembly, where the wood should be trimmed to a thickness of 9mm (⅜in) from its full thickness of 13mm (½in). Re-adjust the fence of the mortise gauge so that the spurs, which had previously measured the width of the grooves, are now set centrally across the thickness of the tongued-and-grooved boards, and scribe a pair of parallel lines along each end-grain.

The two outermost boards must be trimmed so that their width, when assembled to the other boards that make up the panel, projects sufficiently to fit into the 13mm (½in) deep grooves cut in the legs, then scribe lines down their outer edges to denote the marking of the tongues to fit into the leg grooves.

Trim off the waste from the ends of the boards, and from the two outermost edges, with a combination of a sharp-bladed knife, the tenon saw and a 6mm (¼in) chisel, making a trial fitting of the boards within the bed-end assembly.

Before finally assembling the headboard and footboard, drill two 6mm (¼in) holes to each mortise and tenon joint through the side of the mortise and slightly offset through the tenon, to draw-bore the joints with short dowel pegs, thus strengthening the structure. The two holes should be spaced well apart for the top rail joints, but their positions are critical for the bottom rails, since the tenons are quite narrow. Cut sixteen pegs to a length of 32mm (1¼in) each from 6mm (¼in) diameter hardwood dowelling, bevelling the one end by giving a few twists in a pencil sharpener so that the tip of the peg engages with the offset tenon.

Mark a tongue at the end of each board, and remove the waste with the tenon saw, chisel and mallet.

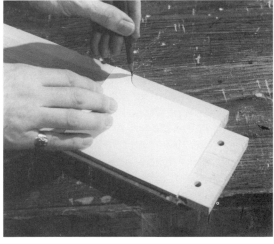

Note the two draw-boring holes drilled through the tenon at one end of the top rail, as a card template is used to mark in the curved decorative shape on the top edge.

Assembling one of the bed-ends.

Mix a quantity of wood glue, apply it by brush to the tongues and grooves of the eleven boards that make up the panelling, joining these together, and then proceed to glue their receiving grooves and the mortises and tenons. Fit the two rails to the panelling, adding the legs, tapping the joints fully home with the mallet and a block of clean scrap wood. Apply a little glue to the dowel pegs, and tap these into their holes, knocking them down as far as they will go. Some of the dowel will remain protruding beyond the surface of the leg, and when the glue has dried and set hard, this may be carefully pared away with the chisel so that the dowel is now flush with the leg.

Finish off the two bed-ends by purchasing four pine door knobs, each measuring approximately 58mm (2¼in) in diameter and 48mm (1⅞in) in length, and drill a 9mm (⅜in) diameter hole into the flat end, at its centre, to a depth of 25mm (1in). Next, stand the assembled headboard and footboard upright, clamped securely in the vice, and use the same 9mm (⅜in) diameter auger bit to bore a hole into the marked centre at the top of each leg, once again drilling to a depth of approximately 25mm (1in). Note that if you intend building two identical beds and installing one on top of the other, in a double-deck arrangement, the holes in the tops of the legs ought to be drilled deeper, to a depth of 38mm (1½in) in which instance the hole will actually pass into the tenon but stop short of the dowel peg used for draw-boring.

A similar hole must also be drilled at the bottom end of each leg in the bed that will be mounted on top. Additional strength can be given to the two interlocked decks by lining the holes with thin metal tubing into which the steel rods fit.

For the wooden knobs, however,

simply cut four 50mm (2in) lengths of 9mm ($\frac{3}{8}$in) hardwood dowelling, gluing one of these into each knob and then, once the glue has dried sufficiently, fit each knob with its protruding dowel pin into the hole at the top of the leg.

Although the bed frame can now be fitted together – the two long rails slotting into the headboard and footboard – it is not yet possible to cut and fit the twelve slats which support the mattress because these have no means of support. The most secure method of mounting the slats between the two long rails is by fitting a notched beam to the inside face of both rails.

Taking each long rail in turn, begin by cutting the beam to a length of 1,914mm (75$\frac{3}{8}$in) from material measuring 70 × 32mm (2$\frac{3}{4}$ × 1$\frac{1}{4}$in) in cross-section. You will notice that the length of the rail, excluding the tenon at each end, is 1,892mm (74$\frac{1}{2}$ in), but a tongue measuring 11mm ($\frac{7}{16}$in) long and 16mm ($\frac{5}{8}$in) wide is marked and cut at both ends of the beam so that when it is attached to the inside of the rail, it fits around the leg and *just* makes contact with the bottom rail of the bed-end, thus providing greater firmness to the assembled bed.

Measure and mark the twelve notches for the slats along the top edge of the

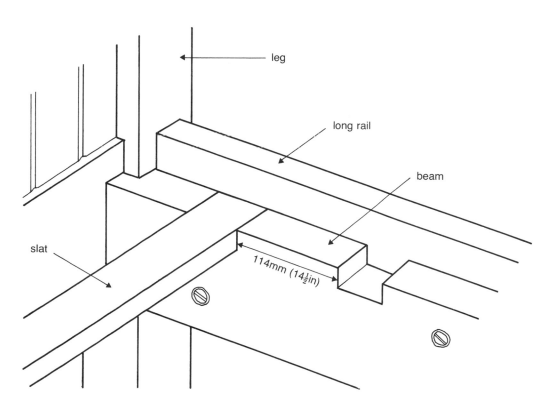

The slats are supported by the beam, which is itself screwed to the inside of the rail.

beam, setting these at regular intervals. Each notch measures 45mm (1¾in) long and 19mm (¾in) deep. Square a pair of pencil lines across the edge and around both sides to indicate the ends of the notches: the first and twelfth notches are set 60mm (2⅜in) from the ends of their respective neighbouring tongues, and there should be a gap of 114mm (4½in) between all of the remaining notches. These measurements are approximate and you are advised to mark them in very lightly with the pencil to begin with, adjusting where necessary in order to create a regularly spaced arrangement, before squaring in the lines.

Set the marking gauge to a distance of 19mm (¾in) between the spur and the fence and scribe a line on both faces between each pair of squared pencil lines to mark in the depth of the notches. Then hold the beam steady on the workbench and cut down on the waste side of all the pencil lines with the tenon saw, working the saw-blade as far as the scribed depth line.

Chop out the waste from each notch with the chisel and mallet.

Chop out the waste with the 19mm (¾in) chisel and mallet, cutting carefully from both sides of the beam, starting about halfway down the depth of the notch, and cutting closer and closer to the scribed line as more and more waste is removed. Finally, check that the notch has been prepared to the correct size by attempting to fit a piece of 45 × 19mm (1¾ × ¾in) material into it. If you have taken sufficient care with your measuring and marking, and cut accurately, there should be no question of the notch being too big; but often it is all too easy to cut it not quite large enough, in which case the ends must be pared lightly with the chisel until the sample length of slat material just slots into place.

When all twelve notches have been successfully cut in both beams, the time

When all twelve notch positions have been marked on the beam, cut down to the scribed depth line with the tenon saw.

A tongue is cut at each end of the notched beam, to fit around the leg and thus provide additional strength.

Seven screw-holes are drilled at regular intervals along the length of the beam to attach it to the long rail.

has come for each of the beams to be joined to the inside face of its supporting long rail. Firstly, mark seven screw-hole positions in each beam, spacing these at regular intervals, and alternating them so that one screw-hole is set with its centre 25mm (1in) from the bottom edge of the beam and the next screw-hole is placed 19mm (¾in) from the top edge, and so on, back and forth. Drill out the holes with a No. 10 drill bit, and countersink deeply so that each screw will be set well beneath the surface.

Align the beam against the inside face of the long rail, their bottom edges perfectly flush with each other and their ends corresponding. Clamp them firmly together at both ends so that they cannot slip out of alignment, and mark the screw-hole positions by driving a No. 10 countersunk mild steel woodscrew into each of the seven holes until it pierces the long rail.

Remove the clamps, take away the beam and drill a little way into the long rail with the same No. 10 drill-bit. Finally, screw the two long pieces of wood together with seven 38mm (1½in) No. 10 woodscrews. There is no need to apply wood glue to the abutting surfaces.

Obviously the long rails cannot be glued into the headboard and footboard, otherwise it would never be possible to dismantle the bed and move it any-

where. So the mortise and tenon joints are fastened with a nut-and-bolt arrangement: the mortise and the tenon are both fitted with a special pronged tee-nut into which a round-headed bolt is screwed, thus fastening the two parts of the joint firmly together.

Start by marking the centre of the 6mm (¼in) hole that needs to be drilled through the side of the mortise and into the tenon, setting it 16mm (⅝in) from the edge of the leg in which the mortise has been cut. Drill a shallow 19mm (¾in) diameter

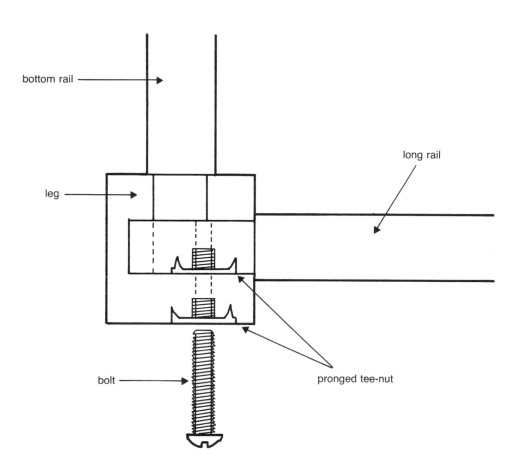

Fix the long rails to the legs with a pronged tee-nut.

A hole is carefully measured and drilled through the side of the long rail mortise to receive a pronged tee-nut used to fasten the joint together. A similar nut is embedded in a corresponding position in the tenon. When the bed is assembled, a round-headed bolt is screwed into both nuts.

hole with a suitable centre bit in this position on the leg, taking out waste to a depth of no more than 2mm ($\frac{3}{32}$in), and continue drilling right through the side

of the mortise with the 6mm ($\frac{1}{4}$in) diameter auger bit.

Fit the tenon of the long rail fully into the mortise and, holding it firmly in position, repeat the process of drilling through the mortise hole with the same 6mm ($\frac{1}{4}$in) auger bit so that on this occasion it also bores right through the tenon. Dismantle the rail from the bed-end, and drill another shallow 19mm ($\frac{3}{4}$in) diameter hole in the side of the tenon that corresponds to the outside surface of the leg, once again taking out no more than 2mm ($\frac{3}{32}$in) of waste.

Slightly enlarge each of the holes in the side of the mortise and through the tenon, using the tip of a circular rat-tail file, or some such similar article, until both holes are just large enough to receive a pronged tee-nut; tap each tee-nut fully into place. Now, when the rail is fitted to the bed-end, the joint will be permanently fastened simply by screwing in a 38mm ($1\frac{1}{2}$in) bolt with a 6mm ($\frac{1}{4}$in) diameter thread.

Assemble the two long rails to the headboard and footboard, cut twelve 45 × 19mm ($1\frac{3}{4}$ × $\frac{3}{4}$in) slats to fit in between and drop these into their notches. The bed is finished, apart from having to be sandpapered thoroughly and given several coats of clear varnish.

INDEX